WISC

Preparation Book

Improve Your

WISC®-V

Test-Taking Skills

With 160 Exercises

Zoe Hampton

Other IQ books by the author
https://prfc.nl/go/amznbooks

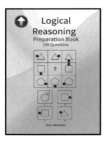

Our Mobile Applications for IQ Training

https://prfc.nl/go/allapps

Follow us on social media

Web site: https://prfc.nl/go/pc

Facebook: https://prfc.nl/go/fbpc

Instagram: https://prfc.nl/go/inpc

LinkedIn: https://prfc.nl/go/lipc

YouTube: https://prfc.nl/go/ytpc

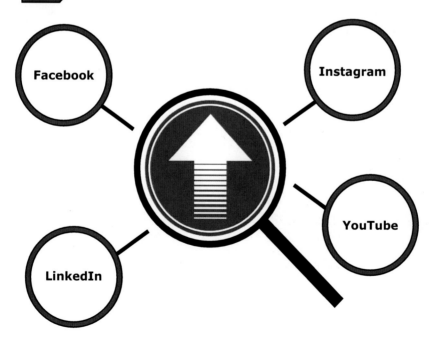

Table of Contents

Introduction   7

Picture Concepts Subtest   8

Pattern Matrix Reasoning Subtest   49

Naming Speed Literacy Subtest   90

Naming Speed Quantity Subtest   102

Immediate Symbol Translation Subtest   113

Delayed Symbol Translation Subtest   134

Recognition Symbol Translation Subtest   138

Digit Span Forward Subtest   146

Digit Span Backward Subtest   148

Digit Span Sequencing Subtest   150

Letter - Number Sequencing Subtest   152

Picture Span Subtest   156

Answers   185

Introduction

WISC®-V Test Preparation Book

The Wechsler Intelligence Scale for Children®/WISC® is used to assess intelligence in children aged 6 to 16. It consists of 16 primary and five complementary subtests. The WISC®-V assessment takes between 50 and 65 minutes to complete. The purpose of the test is to determine whether or not the child is gifted, as well as the student's cognitive strengths and weaknesses.

This practice book includes exercises for one of the new primary subtests, the Picture Span Subtest.

About this book

This preparation book consists 160 exercises (suitable for children aged 6 to 16), subtest instructions and answer key with detailed explanations. These exercises will help you improve your WISC®-V test-taking skills. The book contains exercises from the following Primary and Secondary subtests:

- Picture Concepts
- Pattern Matrix Reasoning
- Naming Speed Literacy & Naming Speed Quantity
- Symbol Translation
- Digit Span
- Picture Span

Picture Concepts Subtest
40 questions

Picture Concepts assesses categorical and abstract reasoning abilities. Children are asked to examine two (or three) rows of pictured objects and point to the one from each row that has a characteristic in common with the one (or two) from the other row(s). Picture Concepts is a non-timed subtest that gets increasingly difficult.

Instructions:

1. Tell the child to look at the pictures.
2. Say to the child: "You must select one image from the first row, one image from the second row, and one image from the third row (for questions with three rows). All three of the images you chose have something in common."
3. After the child has selected a picture from each row, you can inquire as to how the selected images are related.

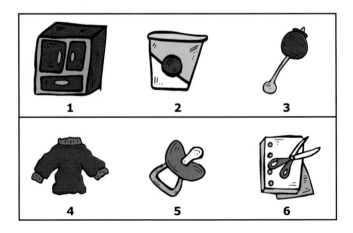

Answer on page 185

Question 1
Picture concepts

A: 3, 5

B: 1, 6

C: 2, 4

D: 4, 6

Question 2
Picture concepts

A: 2, 6

B: 1, 5

C: 4, 6

D: 3, 5

Answer on page 185

Question 3
Picture concepts

A: | 3, 4

B: | 1, 6

C: | 2, 5

D: | 1, 4

Answer on page 185

Question 4
Picture concepts

A: 2, 4   B: 4, 6

C: 3, 5   D: 3, 4

Answer on page 185

Question 5
Picture concepts

A: 2, 4 B: 3, 5

C: 1, 6 D: 1, 5

Answer on page 185

Question 6
Picture concepts

A: 3, 6   B: 1, 5

C: 2, 5   D: 2, 4

Answer on page 185

Question 7
Picture concepts

A: | 1, 5

B: | 2, 4

C: | 3, 4

D: | 1, 6

Question 8
Picture concepts

A: 1, 5

B: 2, 3

C: 1, 6

D: 2, 4

Question 9
Picture concepts

A: | 2, 5

B: | 1, 5

C: | 3, 4

D: | 3, 6

Answer on page 185

Question 10
Picture concepts

A: 1, 4   B: 3, 4

C: 2, 5   D: 1, 3

Answer on page 185

Question 11
Picture concepts

A: 3, 4

B: 1, 6

C: 1, 5

D: 3, 6

Answer on page 185

Question 12
Picture concepts

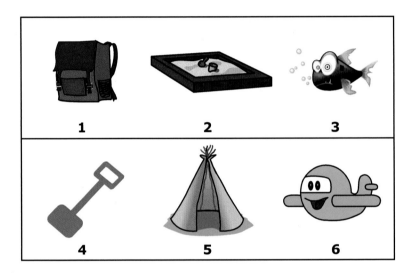

A: 1, 4   B: 3, 6

C: 2, 5   D: 2, 4

Answer on page 185

Question 13
Picture concepts

A: | 3, 4

B: | 2, 6

C: | 1, 5

D: | 4, 6

Answer on page 185

Question 14
Picture concepts

A: 1, 5

B: 3, 6

C: 2, 4

D: 1, 6

Question 15
Picture concepts

A: 2, 5   B: 3, 4

C: 1, 6   D: 1, 4

Question 16
Picture concepts

A: 2, 6   B: 3, 4

C: 3, 5   D: 1, 5

Answer on page 185

Question 17
Picture concepts

A: 1, 4

B: 3, 5

C: 2, 5

D: 1, 6

Question 18
Picture concepts

A: | 1, 5

B: | 3, 6

C: | 2, 4

D: | 1, 6

Answer on page 185

Question 19
Picture concepts

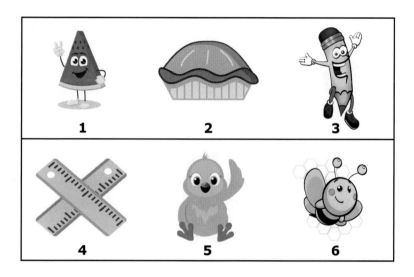

A: | 1, 5

B: | 2, 6

C: | 3, 4

D: | 3, 5

Answer on page 185

Question 20
Picture concepts

<table>
<tr><td>A:</td><td>1, 6</td><td>B:</td><td>3, 4</td></tr>
<tr><td>C:</td><td>2, 5</td><td>D:</td><td>1, 5</td></tr>
</table>

Answer on page 185

Question 21
Picture concepts

A: | 1, 6, 7

B: | 2, 5, 8

C: | 3, 5, 9

D: | 3, 5, 7

Answer on page 185

Question 22
Picture concepts

A: 2, 4, 8

B: 1, 6, 7

C: 3, 5, 9

D: 1, 4, 8

Answer on page 185

Question 23
Picture concepts

A: | 1, 5, 8

B: | 3, 6, 7

C: | 2, 6, 9

D: | 2, 4, 9

31

Answer on page 185

Question 24
Picture concepts

A: | 3, 5, 7

B: | 2, 6, 8

C: | 1, 4, 9

D: | 3, 4, 6

Answer on page 185

Question 25
Picture concepts

A: | 1, 4, 9

B: | 3, 5, 9

C: | 2, 6, 8

D: | 3, 5, 8

33

Question 26
Picture concepts

A: 2, 6, 8

B: 3, 4, 7

C: 1, 5, 9

D: 1, 6, 9

Answer on page 185

Question 27
Picture concepts

A: 3, 4, 7

B: 2, 6, 8

C: 1, 5, 9

D: 3, 4, 9

Answer on page 185

Question 28
Picture concepts

A: 3, 5, 7

B: 2, 4, 8

C: 1, 6, 8

D: 1, 4, 9

Answer on page 185

Question 29
Picture concepts

A: 3, 4, 9   B: 1, 6, 7

C: 2, 4, 7   D: 2, 5, 8

Answer on page 185

Question 30
Picture concepts

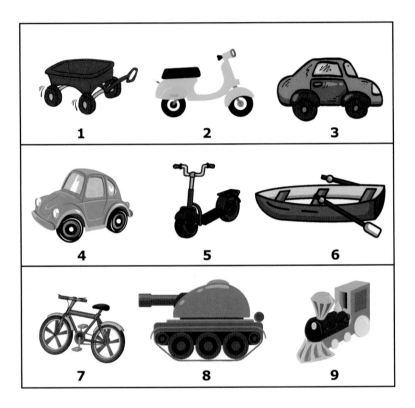

A: 1, 4, 8

B: 2, 5, 7

C: 3, 6, 9

D: 1, 5, 9

Answer on page 186

Question 31
Picture concepts

A: | 2, 5, 7

B: | 1, 6, 8

C: | 3, 5, 8

D: | 3, 4, 9

Question 32
Picture concepts

A: 1, 5, 9   B: 2, 6, 7

C: 3, 4, 8   D: 1, 4, 7

Answer on page 186

Question 33
Picture concepts

A: 3, 4, 7   B: 1, 6, 9

C: 3, 5, 9   D: 2, 6, 8

Answer on page 186

Question 34
Picture concepts

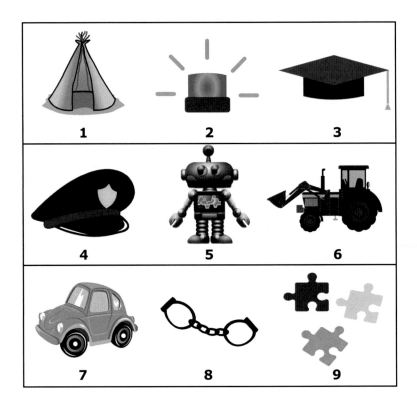

1	2	3
4	5	6
7	8	9

A: 1, 5, 9

B: 2, 4, 8

C: 3, 4, 7

D: 1, 6, 7

Answer on page 186

Question 35
Picture concepts

A: 2, 6, 9   B: 1, 6, 8

C: 3, 5, 7   D: 3, 4, 7

Question 36
Picture concepts

A: 3, 5, 9

B: 1, 6, 8

C: 2, 6, 7

D: 2, 4, 8

Answer on page 186

Question 37
Picture concepts

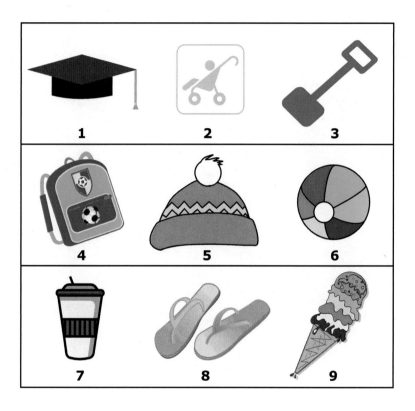

A: | 3, 6, 8   B: | 1, 4, 7

C: | 2, 5, 9   D: | 1, 5, 8

Question 38
Picture concepts

A: 3, 4, 8

B: 2, 5, 9

C: 2, 6, 7

D: 1, 5, 9

Answer on page 186

Question 39
Picture concepts

A: 1, 5, 8

B: 2, 6, 7

C: 3, 4, 9

D: 2, 4, 9

Answer on page 186

Question 40
Picture concepts

A: 1, 4, 9   B: 2, 5, 8

C: 2, 6, 7   D: 3, 4, 9

Pattern Matrix Reasoning Subtest
40 questions

These questions test the ability to complete a shape or figure-based matrix by adding the missing piece. The child must deduce the relationship between the shapes and figures and choose the answer that follows the same rule or completes a pattern. These are questions about cognition or thinking.

Instructions:

1. Tell the child to look at the shapes and figures.
2. Say to the child: "Replace the question mark with the correct shape or figure."
3. After the child has selected a shape or figure, you can inquire as to why he thinks the one he/she has chosen is appropriate.

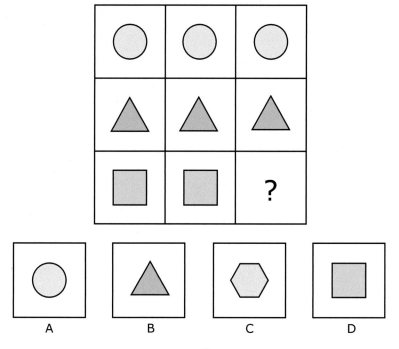

Answer on page 187

Question 41
Pattern Matrix Reasoning

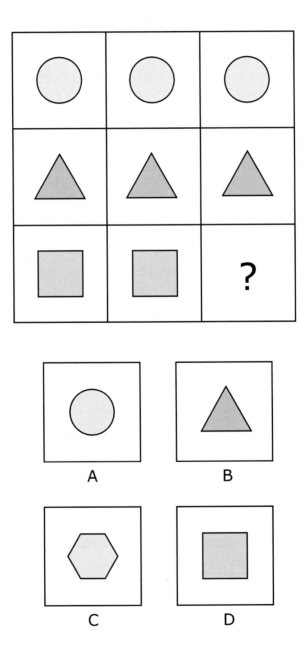

Answer on page 187

Question 42
Pattern Matrix Reasoning

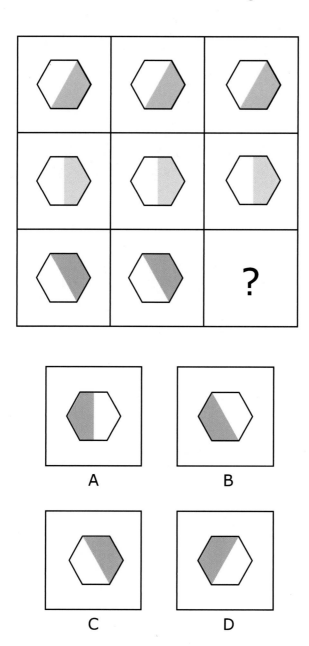

Answer on page 187

Question 43
Pattern Matrix Reasoning

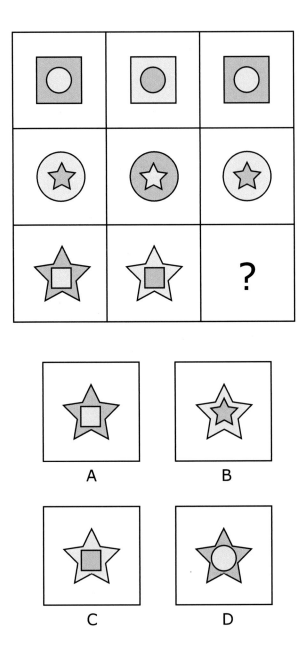

Answer on page 187

Question 44
Pattern Matrix Reasoning

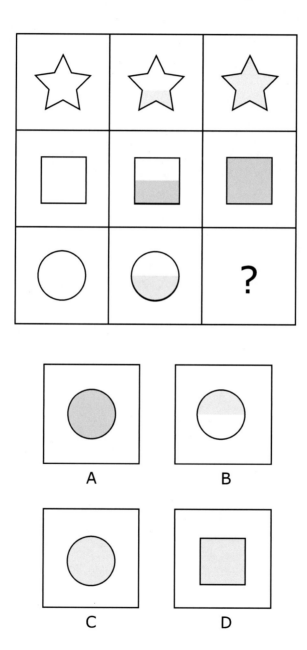

Question 45
Pattern Matrix Reasoning

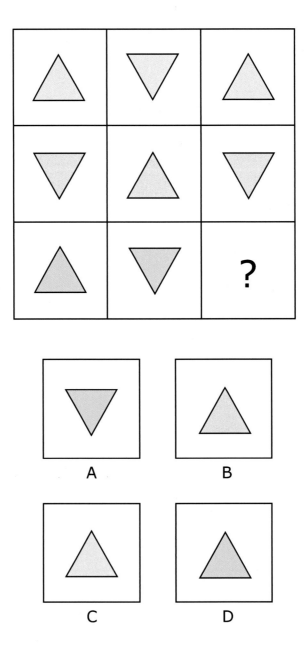

Answer on page 187

Question 46
Pattern Matrix Reasoning

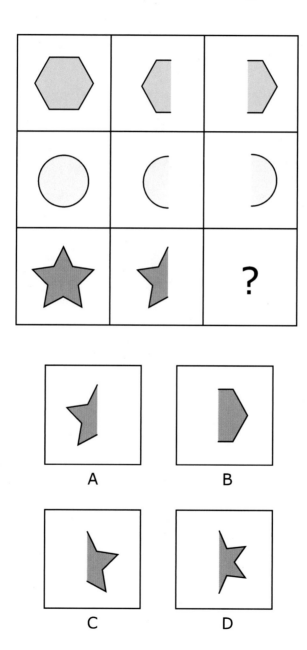

Answer on page 187

Question 47
Pattern Matrix Reasoning

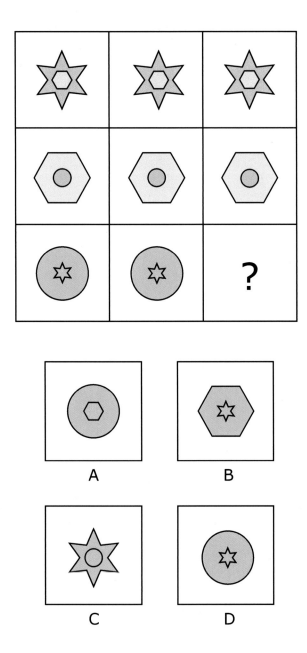

Answer on page 187

Question 48
Pattern Matrix Reasoning

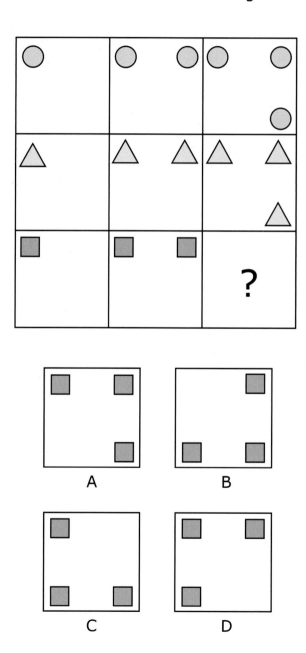

A

B

C

D

Answer on page 187

Question 49
Pattern Matrix Reasoning

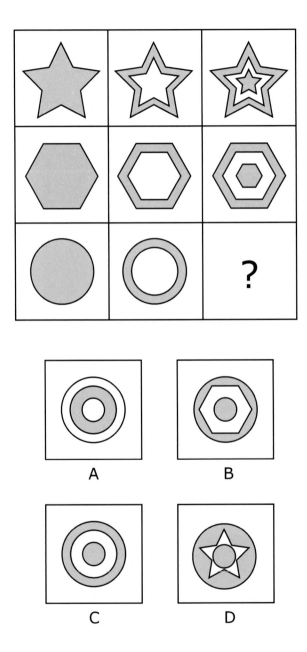

Answer on page 187

Question 50
Pattern Matrix Reasoning

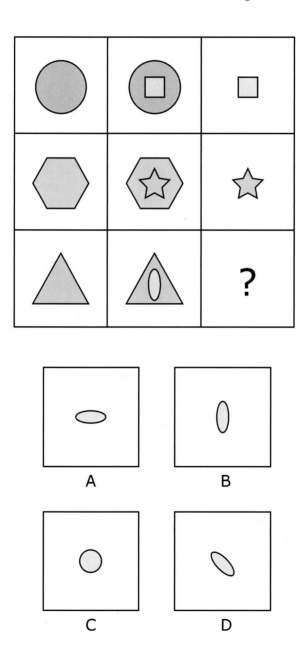

Question 51
Pattern Matrix Reasoning

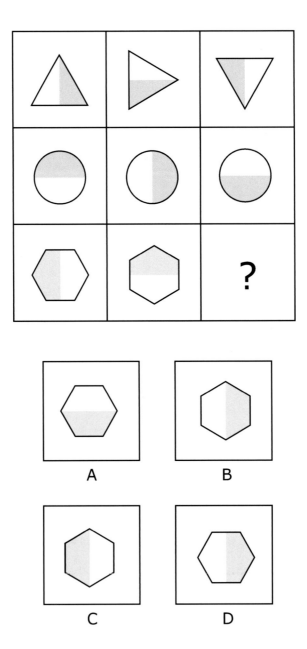

Question 52
Pattern Matrix Reasoning

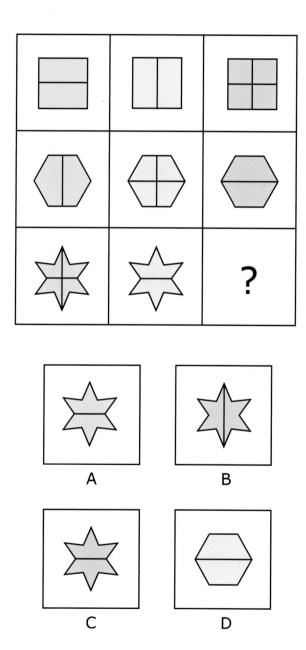

Answer on page 187

Question 53
Pattern Matrix Reasoning

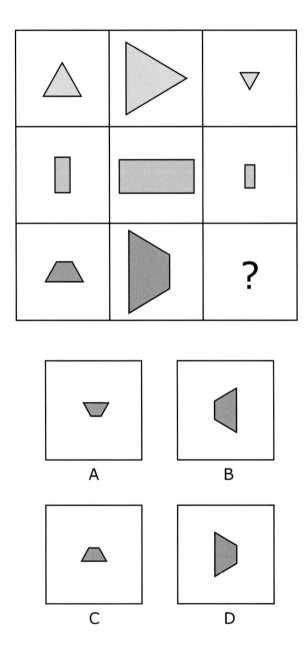

Answer on page 187

Question 54
Pattern Matrix Reasoning

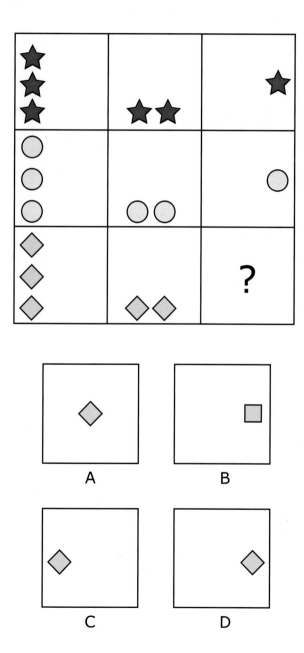

A

B

C

D

Question 55
Pattern Matrix Reasoning

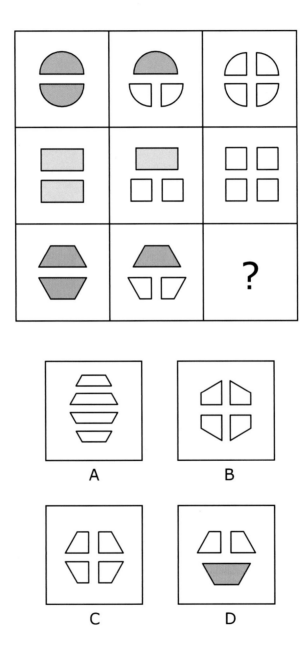

Question 56
Pattern Matrix Reasoning

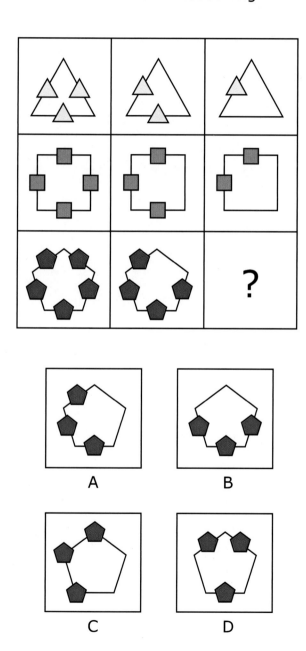

Answer on page 187

Question 57
Pattern Matrix Reasoning

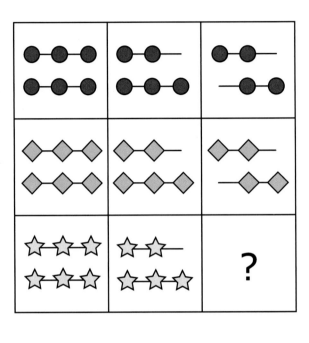

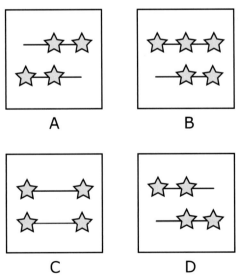

A   B

C   D

Question 58
Pattern Matrix Reasoning

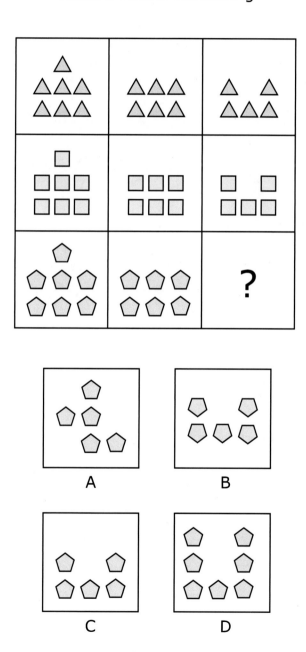

Answer on page 188

Question 59
Pattern Matrix Reasoning

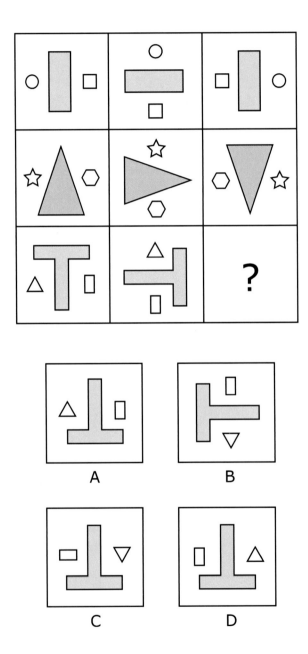

Question 60
Pattern Matrix Reasoning

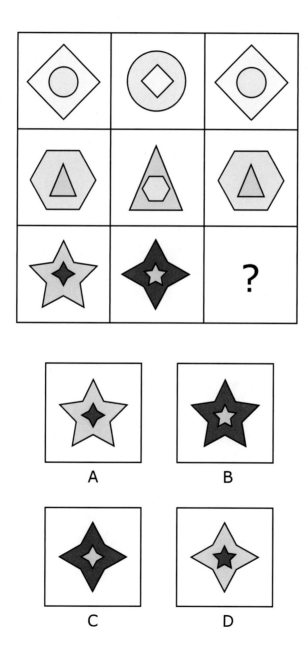

A

B

C

D

Question 61
Pattern Matrix Reasoning

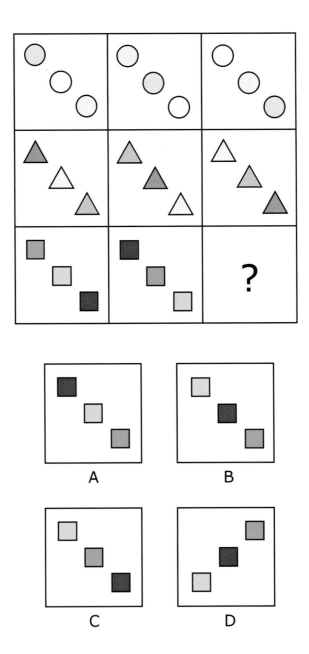

Question 62
Pattern Matrix Reasoning

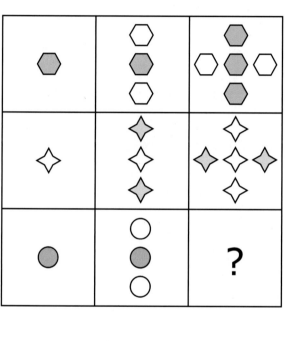

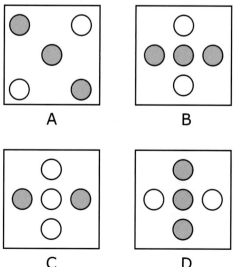

Answer on page 188

Question 63
Pattern Matrix Reasoning

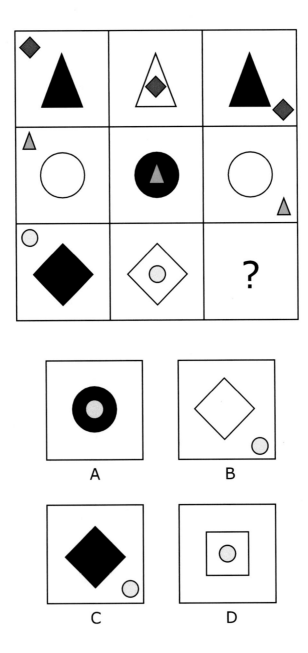

Answer on page 188

Question 64
Pattern Matrix Reasoning

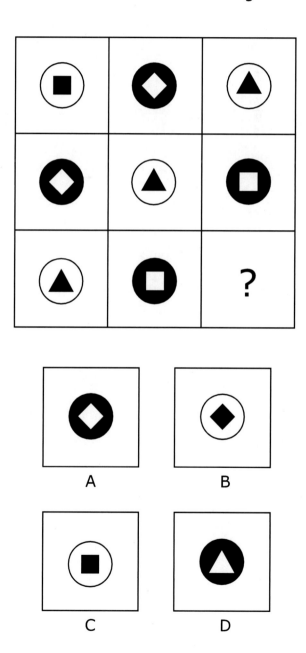

Question 65
Pattern Matrix Reasoning

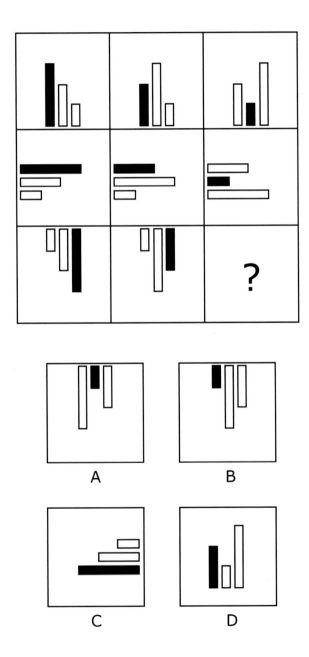

Answer on page 188

Question 66
Pattern Matrix Reasoning

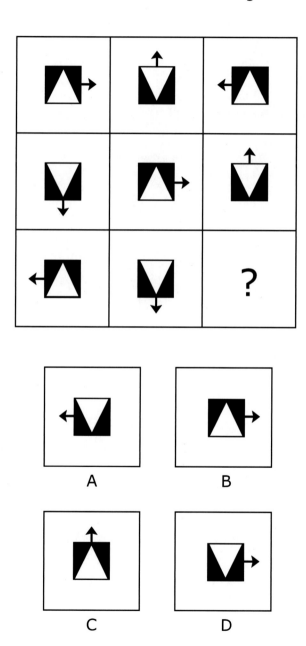

Answer on page 188

Question 67
Pattern Matrix Reasoning

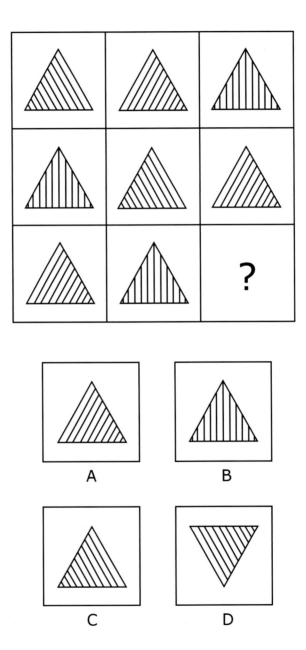

A

B

C

D

Question 68
Pattern Matrix Reasoning

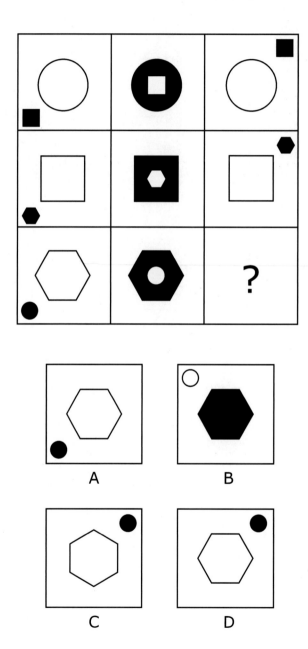

Answer on page 188

Question 69
Pattern Matrix Reasoning

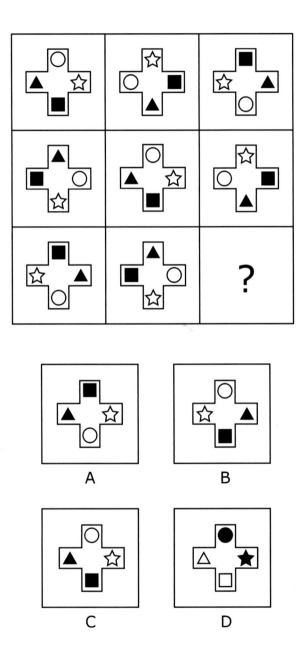

Answer on page 188

Question 70
Pattern Matrix Reasoning

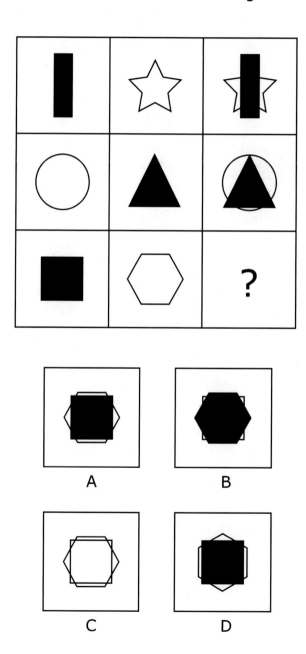

A

B

C

D

Question 71
Pattern Matrix Reasoning

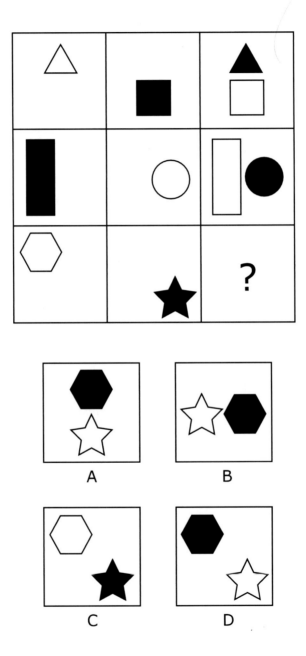

Answer on page 188

Question 72
Pattern Matrix Reasoning

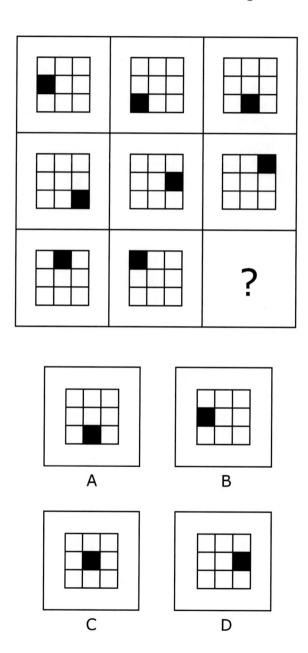

Answer on page 188

Question 73
Pattern Matrix Reasoning

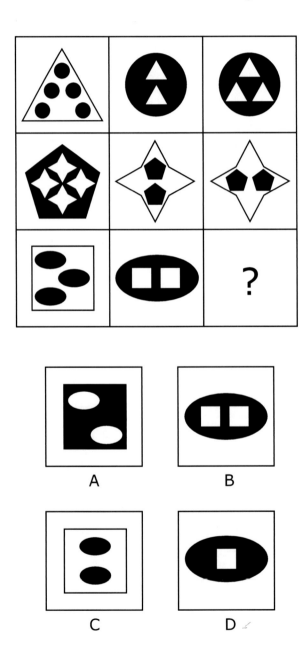

Answer on page 189

Question 74
Pattern Matrix Reasoning

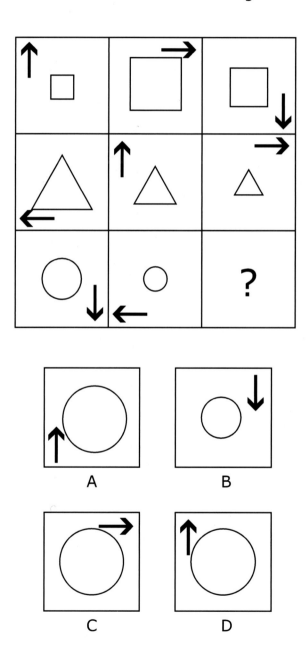

Answer on page 189

Question 75
Pattern Matrix Reasoning

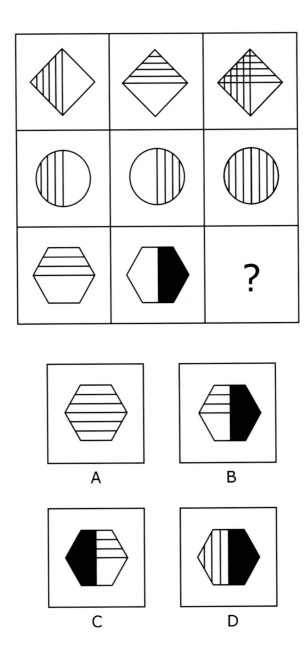

Question 76
Pattern Matrix Reasoning

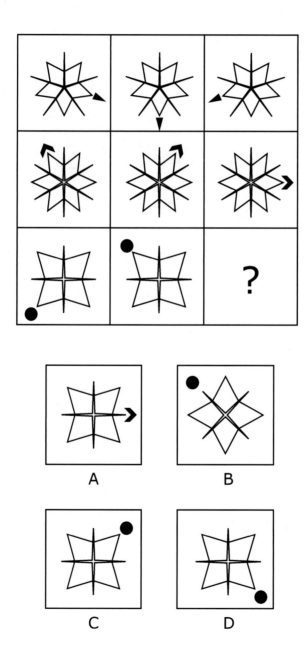

A

B

C

D

Answer on page 189

Question 77
Pattern Matrix Reasoning

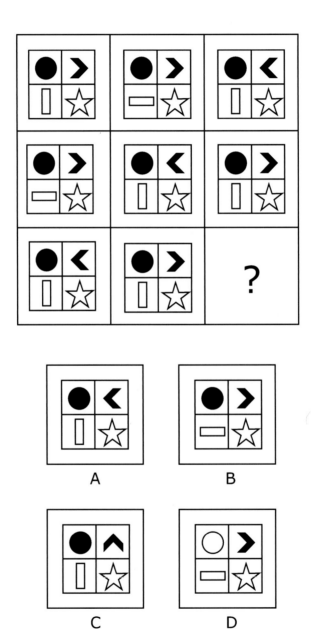

Question 78
Pattern Matrix Reasoning

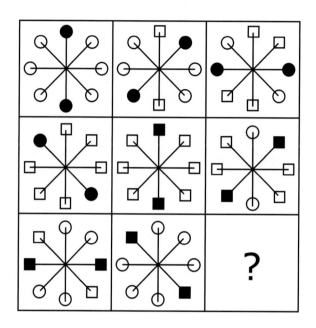

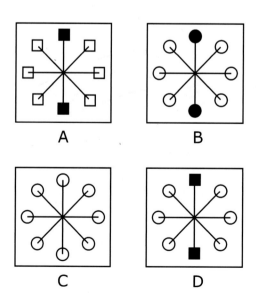

A

B

C

D

Answer on page 189

Question 79
Pattern Matrix Reasoning

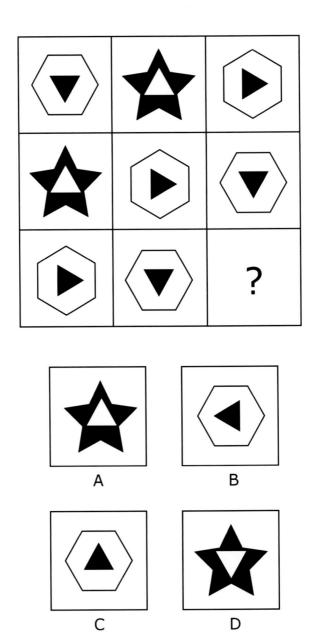

Answer on page 189

Question 80
Pattern Matrix Reasoning

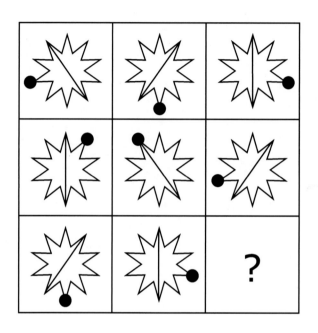

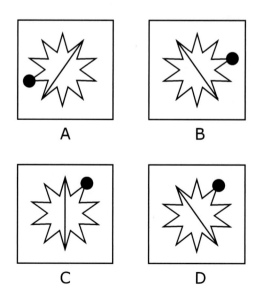

A   B

C   D

Naming Speed Literacy Subtest
10 questions

The Naming Speed Literacy subtest aids in the diagnosis of reading and writing learning disabilities. As quickly as they could during the Naming Speed Literacy subtest, the child named the elements (such as objects of various sizes and colors, letters, and numbers).

Instructions: Questions 81-84

1. Without making any mistakes, say the color and name of each item in each of these rows as quickly as you can. Keep track of your location with your finger.
2. For each set, the child has five minutes.
3. Example: Green frog, blue bird, red tomato, blue car

Instructions: Questions 85-86

1. Without making any mistakes, say the size, color and name of each item in each of these rows as quickly as you can. Keep track of your location with your finger.
2. For each set, the child has five minutes.
3. Example: Big yellow pear, big red tomato, small blue square, big blue dinosaur

Instructions: Questions 87-90

1. As quickly as you can, name the letter and number in each item in each of these rows without making any mistakes. Keep track of your location with your finger.
2. For each set, the child has five minutes.
3. Example: Five, P, W, Eight, One

5 P W 8 1

Question 81
Naming Speed Literacy

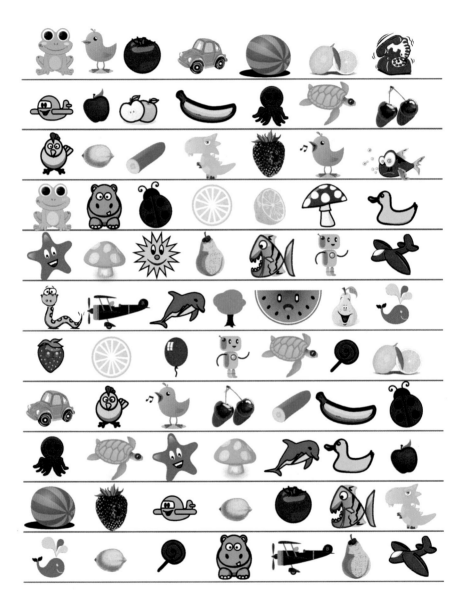

Question 82
Naming Speed Literacy

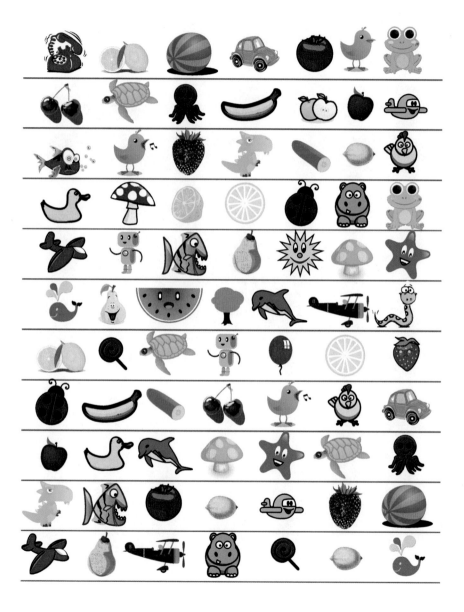

Answer on page 191

Question 83
Naming Speed Literacy

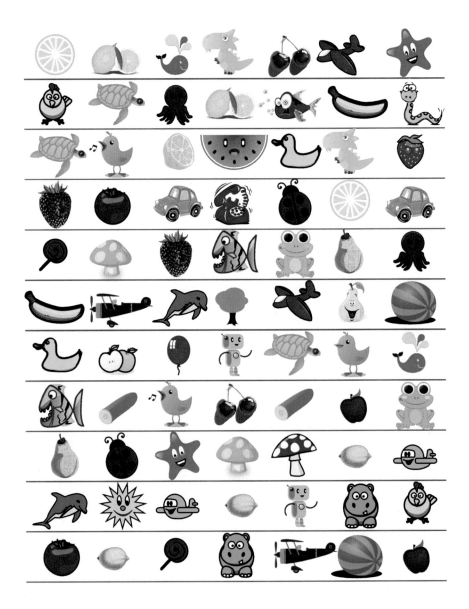

Question 84
Naming Speed Literacy

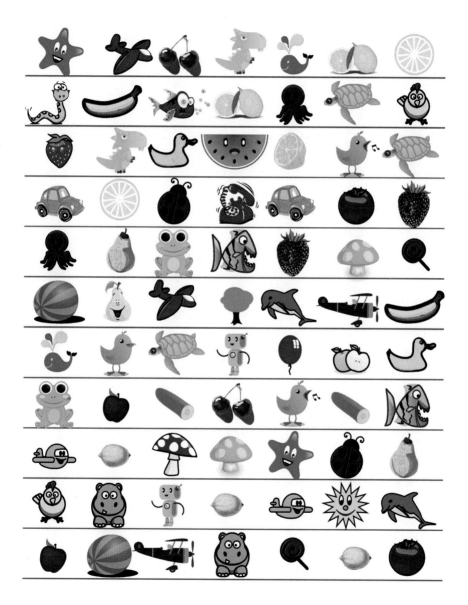

Answer on page 192

Question 85
Naming Speed Literacy

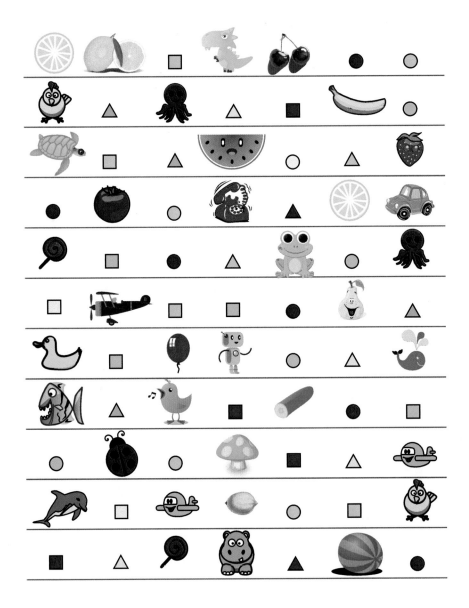

Question 86
Naming Speed Literacy

Answer on page 194

Question 87
Naming Speed Literacy

5 P W 8 1 N S 9 6 4

E A 2 L F 3 7 X C K

6 8 Y D 1 Z 5 U 6 G

J T 4 C O R 7 1 I A

H 2 N M 9 S T 6 P 7

K L 5 1 4 K Q R P 3

F X N 6 M 3 9 K B U

L 6 4 2 W 1 C A 8 4

Q 7 Y 3 P V X 1 6 3

Y C 2 Z I T 3 2 E R

J L F 5 3 7 1 G D S

Answer on page 194

Question 88
Naming Speed Literacy

R S 2 P 5 9 L H G Z

4 6 J T 1 M D 6 C 2

1 Q V 5 N 9 V B 5 9

X 4 E 7 J L W U 6 4

2 9 3 G S 4 Q K 5 U

Z 5 8 T X 6 B 8 N E

K Y P 4 9 1 C S 6 3

J P G I 5 7 D 8 H 1

8 O T P S V 4 2 9 4

K B 9 V 2 Z 7 E M S

6 Q K F 6 8 C Y 1 7

Answer on page 194

Question 89
Naming Speed Literacy

6 P w 5 1 N S 9 6 4

E A 2 L F 3 7 x C K

6 8 Y d 1 Z 2 U 6 G

j T 3 C o R 7 1 i a

h 2 n M 9 S T 6 p 7

k L 5 1 4 K Q r P 2

f X N 6 M 3 8 K b U

l 6 3 2 W 1 C a 8 4

q 7 y 3 P v X 1 6 3

Y C 2 z I T 8 2 e R

J L f 9 3 7 1 g D S

Question 90
Naming Speed Literacy

r S 8 P 5 3 L h g Z

2 6 J T 1 mD 6 C 2

7 q V 5 N 9 V b 6 1

X 4 E 7 J L w U 6 3

5 9 3 g S 7 q K 5 U

Z 5 8 T X 6 B 8 N E

K y P 4 9 1 c S 6 8

J P g I 5 7 d 8 h 1

2 O t P S v 1 2 9 7

K b 9 V 2 z 7 e mS

4 q k f 6 5 C Y 1 9

Naming Speed Quantity Subtest
10 questions

The Naming Speed Quantity subtest requires the child to name the number of items and shapes inside a series of boxes as quickly as possible. This subtest aids in the diagnosis of math-related disabilities.

Instructions: Questions 91-95

1. As quickly as you can, say how many fruit and animals are in each box. Try your best to avoid making any mistakes. Keep track of your location with your finger.
2. For each set, the child has five minutes.
3. Example: 4, 2, 1, 2, 2

Instructions: Questions 96-100

1. As quickly as you can, say how many shapes and figures are in each box. Try your best to avoid making any mistakes. Keep track of your location with your finger.
2. For each set, the child has five minutes.
3. Example: 5, 3, 1, 4

Answer on page 195

Question 91
Naming Speed Quantity

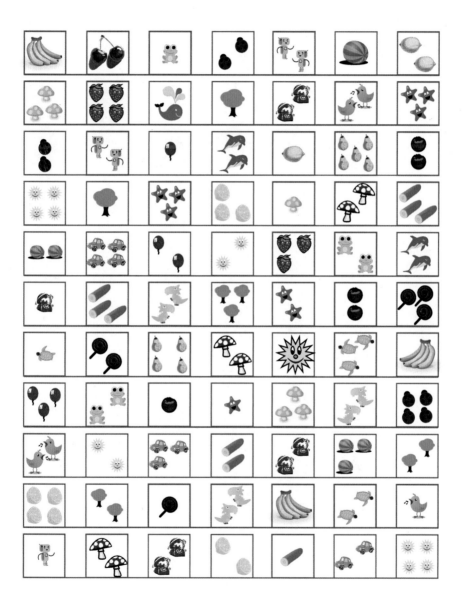

Question 92
Naming Speed Quantity

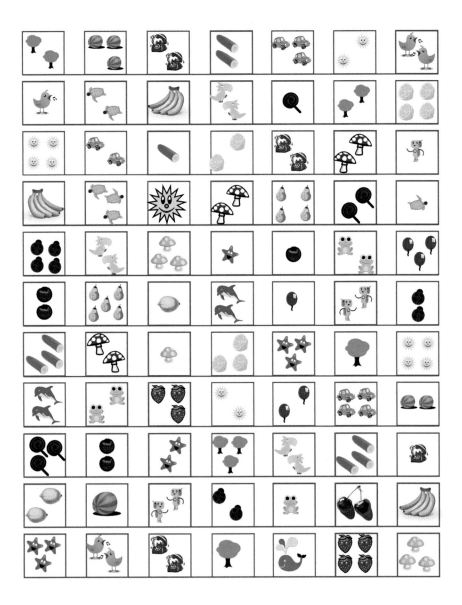

Answer on page 195

Question 93
Naming Speed Quantity

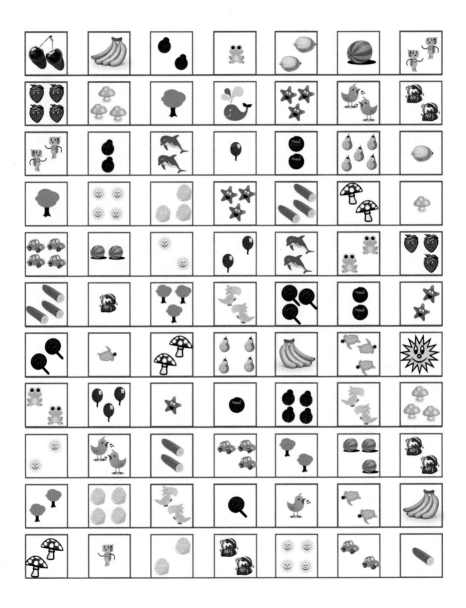

Question 94
Naming Speed Quantity

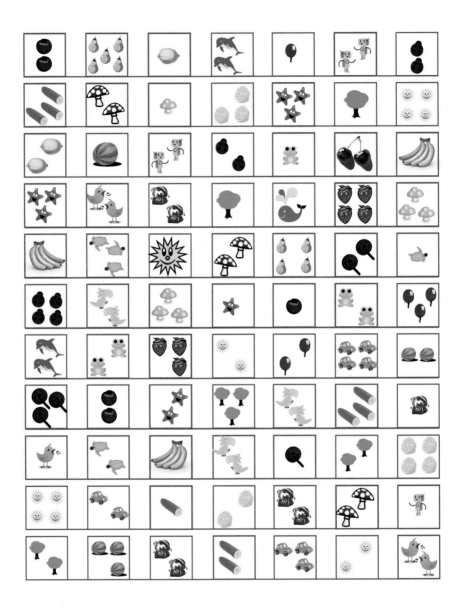

Answer on page 196

Question 95
Naming Speed Quantity

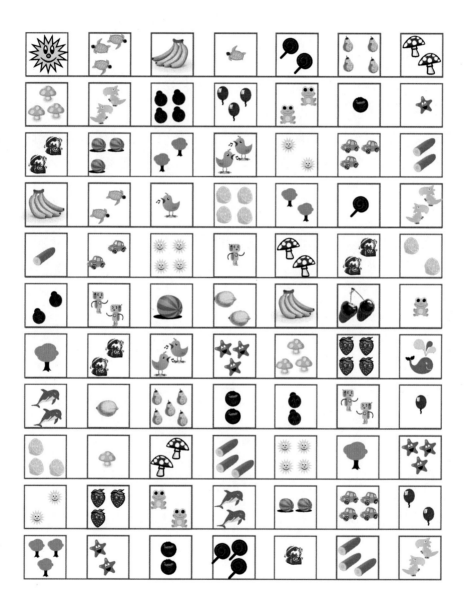

Answer on page 196

Question 96
Naming Speed Quantity

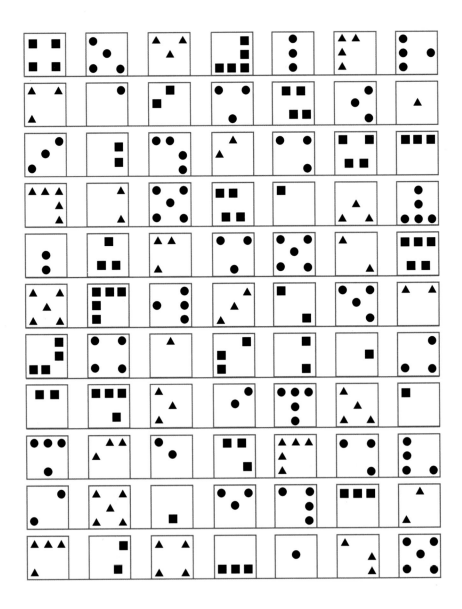

Answer on page 196

Question 97
Naming Speed Quantity

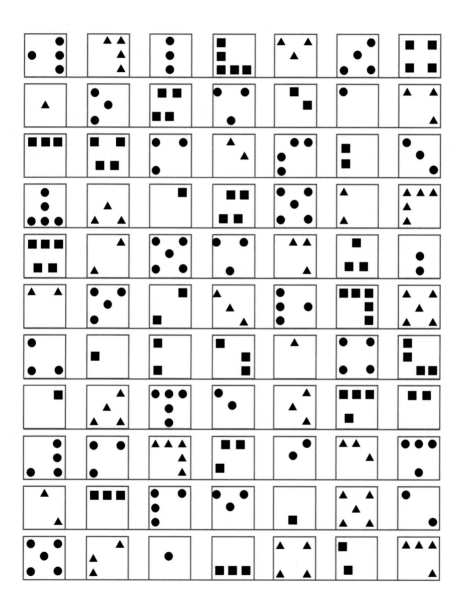

Answer on page 196

Question 98
Naming Speed Quantity

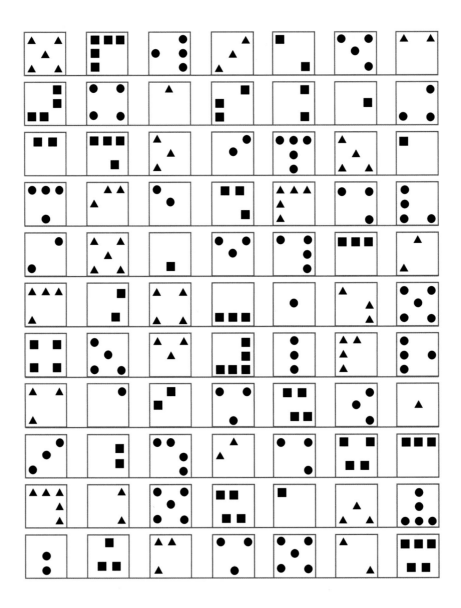

Answer on page 197

Question 99
Naming Speed Quantity

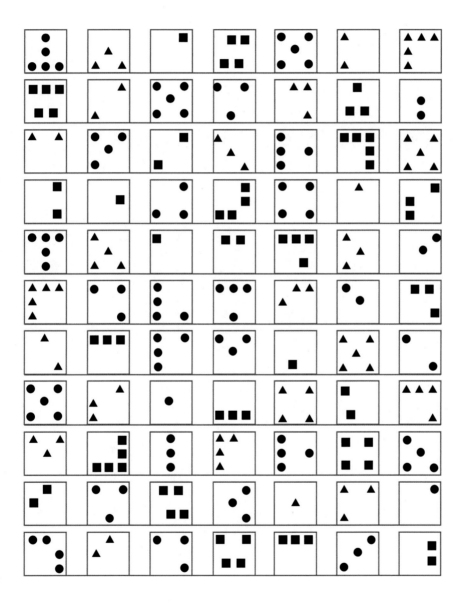

111

Question 100
Naming Speed Quantity

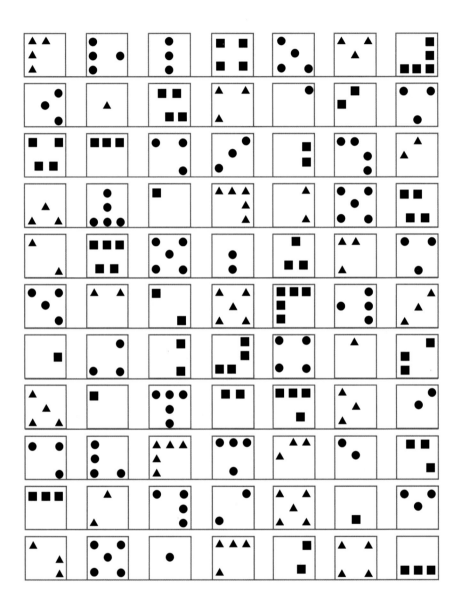

Immediate Symbol Translation Subtest
10 questions

The Symbol Translation subtest measures a child's ability to learn new information. It will be used by psychologists to aid in the diagnosis of disabilities involving information storage and retrieval deficiencies.

Instructions: Questions 101- 110

1. Show the symbols to the child and explain what each one means. Give the child about a minute to try to remember the symbols.
2. Show the child the same symbols, but this time without the text, and ask him to try to remember each one and say its name in the order indicated.
3. Example: You are going to school today.

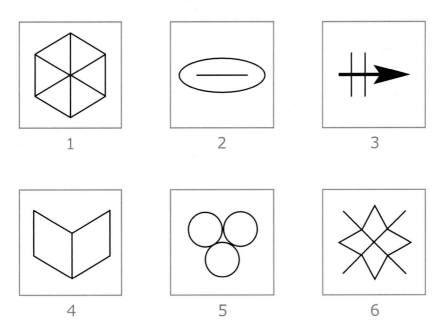

Answer on page 198

Question 101
Immediate Symbol Translation

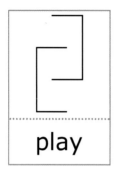

play

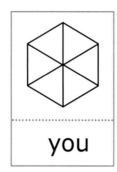

you

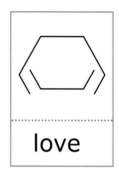

love

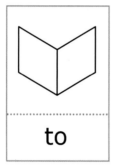

to

golf

114

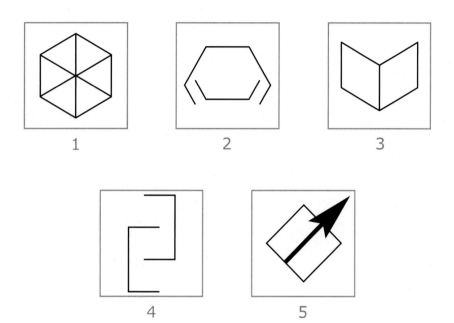

1

2

3

4

5

Answer on page 198

Question 102
Immediate Symbol Translation

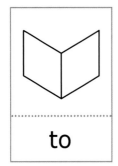

to

like

come

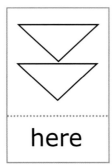

here

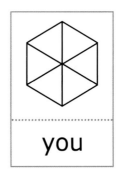

you

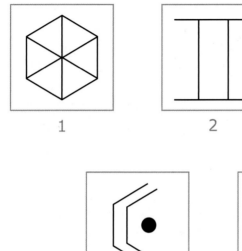

1
2
3

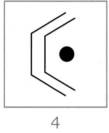

4

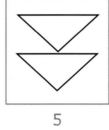

5

Answer on page 198

Question 103
Immediate Symbol Translation

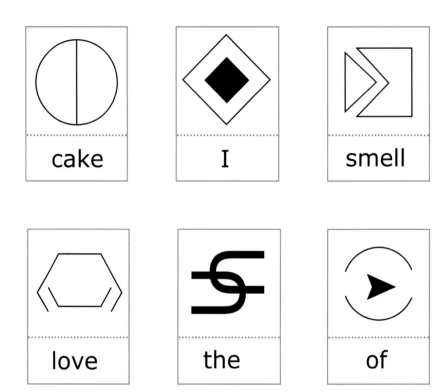

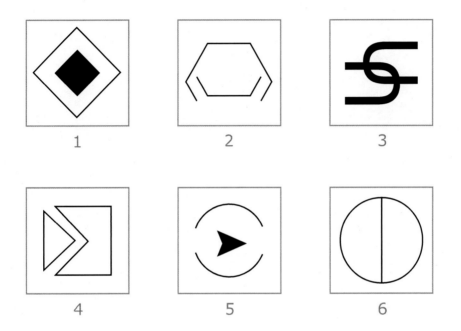

1   2   3

4   5   6

Answer on page 198

Question 104
Immediate Symbol Translation

cook

I

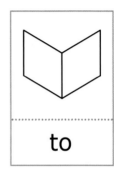

to

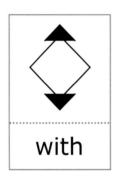

with

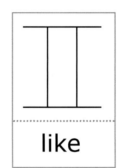

like

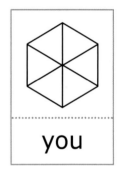

you

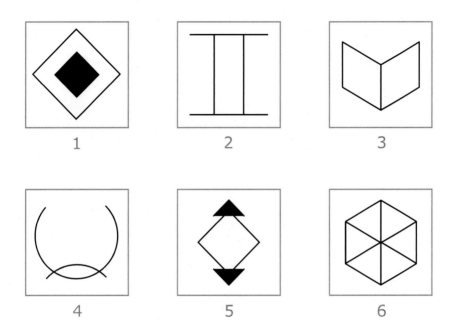

1   2   3

4   5   6

Answer on page 198

Question 105
Immediate Symbol Translation

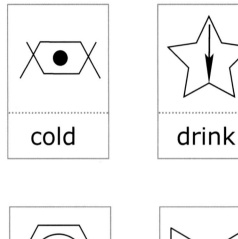

cold

drink

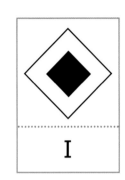

I

water

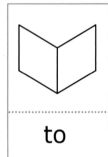

to

like

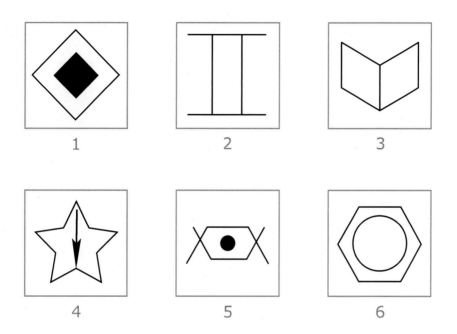

1   2   3

4   5   6

Answer on page 198

Question 106
Immediate Symbol Translation

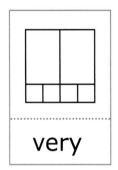

very

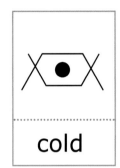

cold

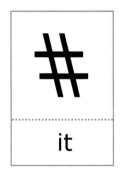

it

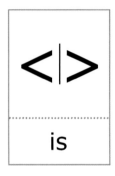

is

today

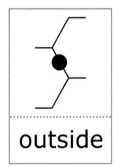

outside

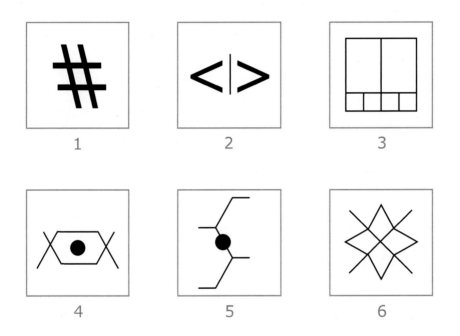

1

2

3

4

5

6

Answer on page 198

Question 107
Immediate Symbol Translation

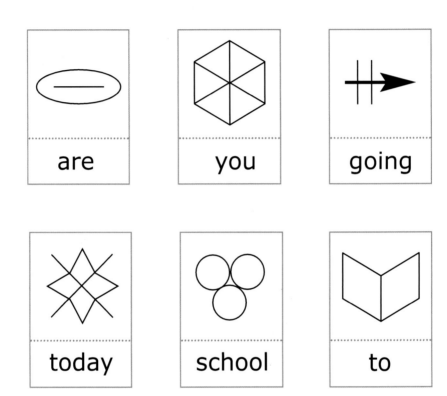

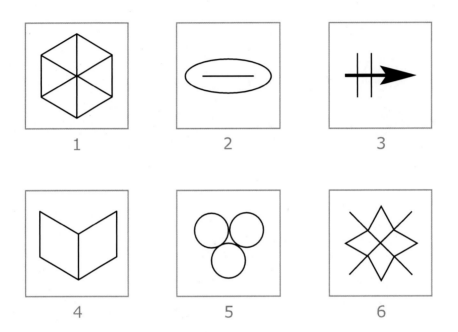

1   2   3

4   5   6

Question 108
Immediate Symbol Translation

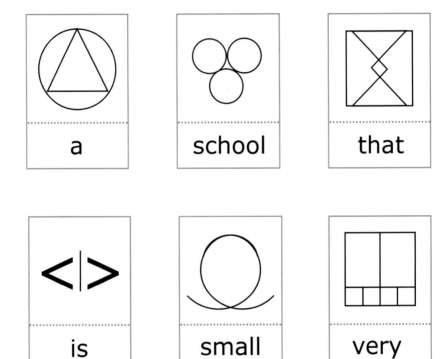

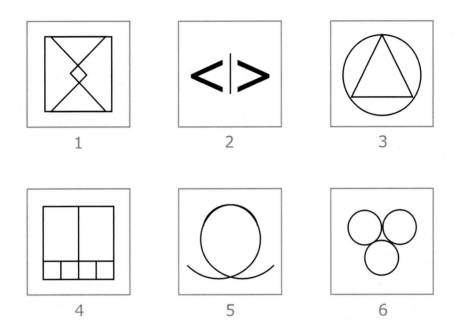

1   2   3

4   5   6

Answer on page 198

Question 109
Immediate Symbol Translation

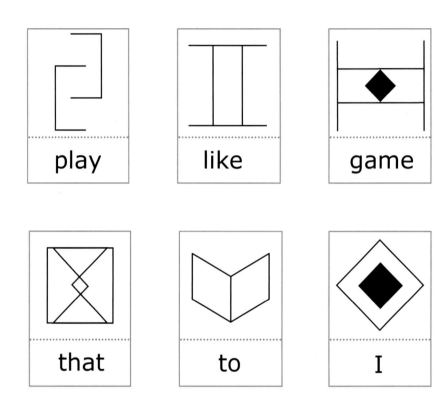

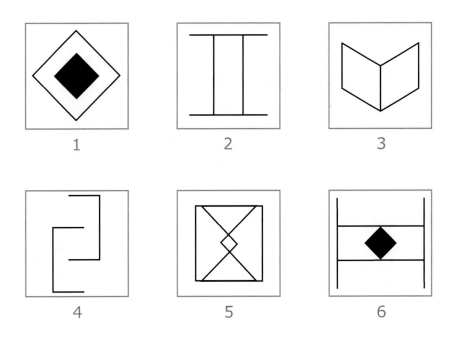

1 2 3

4 5 6

Answer on page 198

Question 110
Immediate Symbol Translation

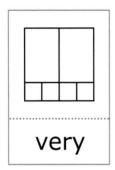

very

ball

small

a

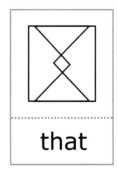

that

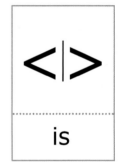

is

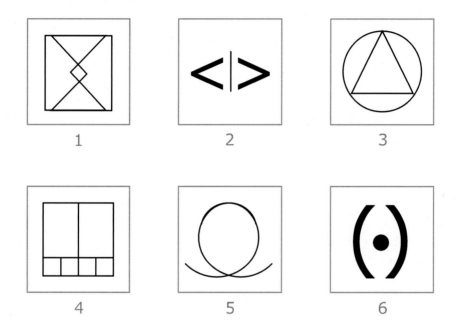

1   2   3

4   5   6

Delayed Symbol Translation Subtest
9 questions

The Symbol Translation subtest measures a child's ability to learn new information. It will be used by psychologists to aid in the diagnosis of disabilities involving information storage and retrieval deficiencies.

Instructions: Questions 111- 119

1. After completing the previous subtest (Immediate Symbol Translation), wait about 30 minutes and ask the child if he/she remembers the learned symbols.
2. Show the child the symbol page and ask him or her to explain what each symbol means.
3. Example: play, love

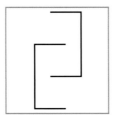 

Question 111
Delayed Symbol Translation

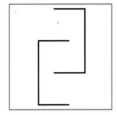 

Question 112
Delayed Symbol Translation

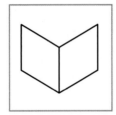 

Question 113
Delayed Symbol Translation

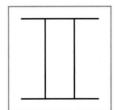 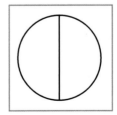

Answer on page 198

Question 114
Delayed Symbol Translation

Question 115
Delayed Symbol Translation

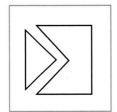 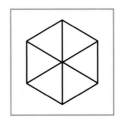 

Question 116
Delayed Symbol Translation

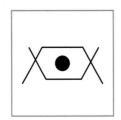  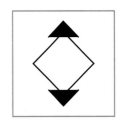

Answer on page 198

Question 117
Delayed Symbol Translation

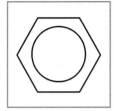 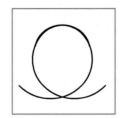 

Question 118
Delayed Symbol Translation

  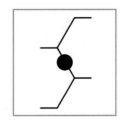

Question 119
Delayed Symbol Translation

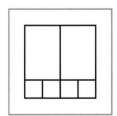 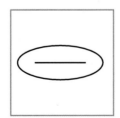 

Recognition Symbol Translation Subtest
21 questions

The Symbol Translation subtest measures a child's ability to learn new information. It will be used by psychologists to aid in the diagnosis of disabilities involving information storage and retrieval deficiencies.

Instructions: Questions 120- 140

1. Ask the child to indicate the meaning of each symbol after finishing the previous test (Delayed Symbol Translation).
2. Show the child the symbol page and ask him or her to explain what each symbol means.
3. Example: golf

A: play   B: golf

C: you   D: love

Question 120
Delayed Recognition

A: **play**   B: **golf**

C: **you**   D: **love**

Question 121
Delayed Recognition

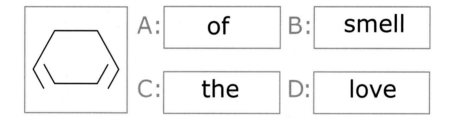

A: **of**   B: **smell**

C: **the**   D: **love**

Question 122
Delayed Recognition

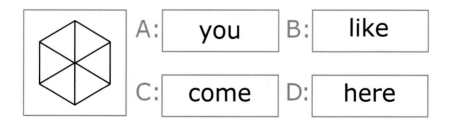

A: **you**   B: **like**

C: **come**   D: **here**

Question 123
Delayed Recognition

A: play   B: love

C: you   D: to

Question 124
Delayed Recognition

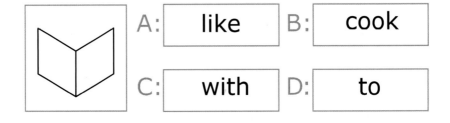

A: like   B: cook

C: with   D: to

Question 125
Delayed Recognition

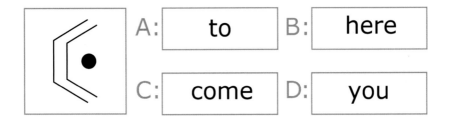

A: to   B: here

C: come   D: you

Answer on page 199

Question 126
Delayed Recognition

A: like   B: here

C: the   D: come

Question 127
Delayed Recognition

A: I   B: cold

C: like   D: water

Question 128
Delayed Recognition

A: the   B: cake

C: smell   D: of

Question 129
Delayed Recognition

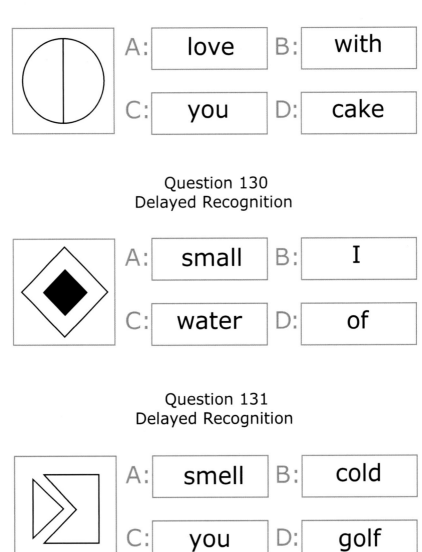

A: love   B: with

C: you   D: cake

Question 130
Delayed Recognition

A: small   B: I

C: water   D: of

Question 131
Delayed Recognition

A: smell   B: cold

C: you   D: golf

Answer on page 199

Question 132
Delayed Recognition

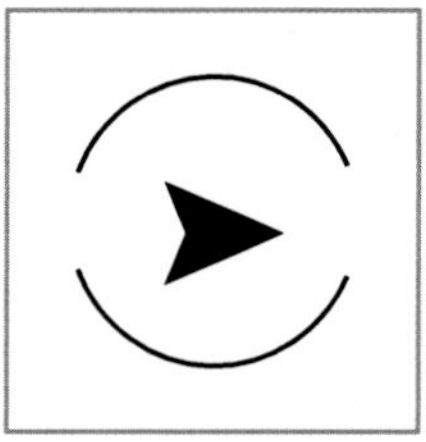

A: the
B: that
C: of
D: ball

Question 133
Delayed Recognition

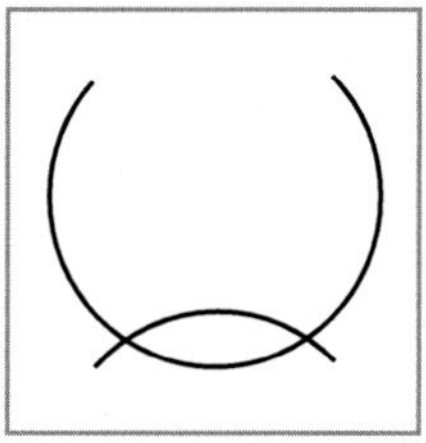

A: cake
B: you
C: like
D: cook

Question 134
Delayed Recognition

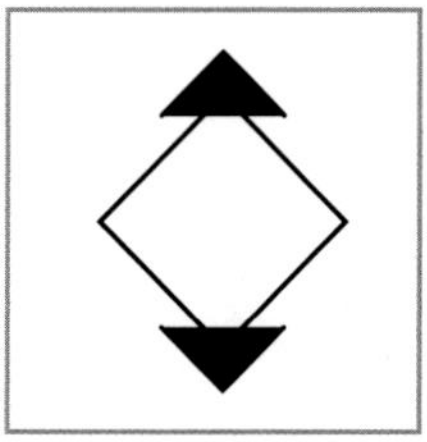

A: with
B: draw
C: love
D: I

Answer on page 199

Question 135
Delayed Recognition

A: like

B: drink

C: of

D: cold

Question 136
Delayed Recognition

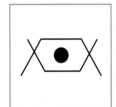

A: cold

B: ball

C: cake

D: you

Question 137
Delayed Recognition

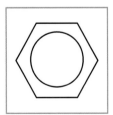

A: love

B: small

C: smell

D: water

Answer on page 199

Question 138
Delayed Recognition

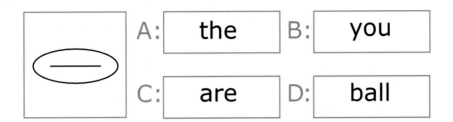

A: the B: you

C: are D: ball

Question 139
Delayed Recognition

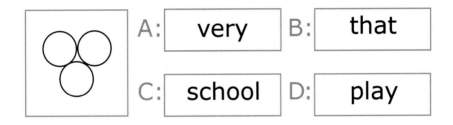

A: very B: that

C: school D: play

Question 140
Delayed Recognition

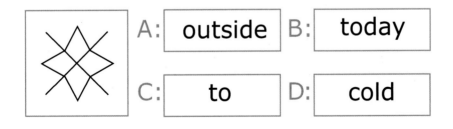

A: outside B: today

C: to D: cold

Digit Span Forward Subtest
1 question

The child is asked to repeat numbers in different orders in the Digit Span subtest. This subtest assesses a child's working auditory memory, or their ability to recall information that was just spoken to them.

Instructions: Question 141

1. Say the first row of numbers and ask the child to repeat them in the same order. Then proceed with the rows that follow.
2. The numbers in the rows will gradually increase.
3. The numbers should not be visible to the child; they should only be heard from you.
4. Example: 1, 4

Answer on page 200

Question 141
Digit Span

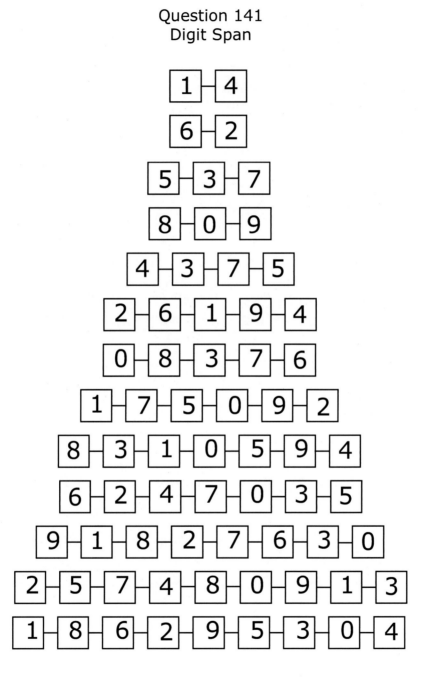

Digit Span Backward Subtest
1 question

The child is asked to repeat numbers in different orders in the Digit Span subtest. This subtest assesses a child's working auditory memory, or their ability to recall information that was just spoken to them.

Instructions: Question 142

1. Say the first row of numbers and then ask the child to repeat them backwards, beginning with the last number. Then proceed with the rows that follow.
2. The numbers in the rows will gradually increase.
3. The numbers should not be visible to the child; they should only be heard from you.
4. Example: 7, 5

Question 142
Digit Span Backwards

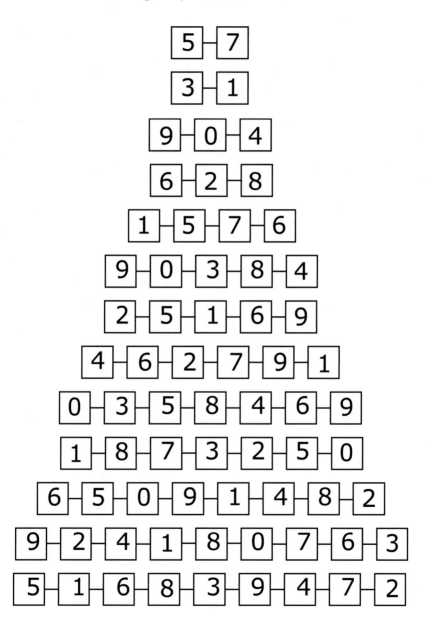

Digit Span Sequencing Subtest
1 question

The child is asked to repeat numbers in different orders in the Digit Span subtest. This subtest assesses a child's working auditory memory, or their ability to recall information that was just spoken to them.

Instructions: Question 143

1. When you say the first row of numbers, have the child repeat them, beginning with the lowest and going up to the highest. Then proceed with the rows that follow.
2. The numbers in the rows will gradually increase.
3. The numbers should not be visible to the child; they should only be heard from you.
4. Example: 4, 5, 8

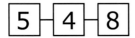

Answer on page 201

Question 143
Digit Span Sequencing

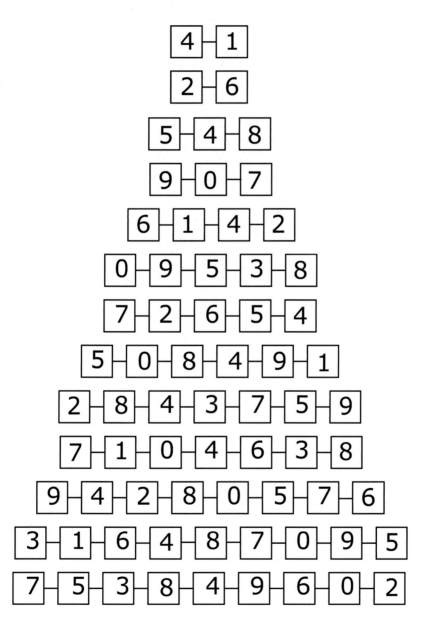

Letter - Number Sequencing Subtest
3 questions

The tester will read a series of numbers and letters during this subtest. The child is asked to remember the numbers ascending and the letters alphabetically. This subtest assesses a child's working auditory memory, or their ability to recall information that was just spoken to them.

Instructions: Questions 144-146

1. When you say the numbers and letters in the row, ask the child to tell you the numbers first in ascending order and then the letters in alphabetical order. Then proceed with the rows that follow.
2. The numbers and letters in the rows will gradually increase.
3. The numbers and letters should not be visible to the child; they should only be heard from you.
4. Example: 2, 9, B, J

Answer on page 201

Question 144
Letter - Number Sequencing

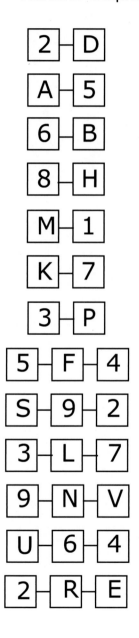

Question 145
Letter - Number Sequencing

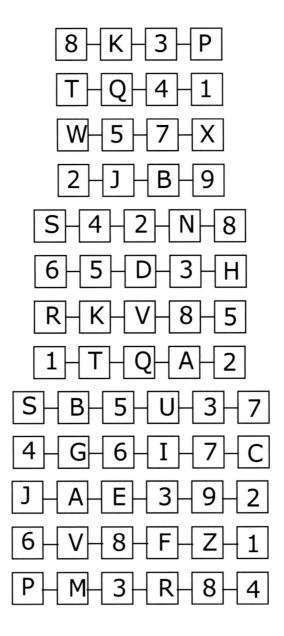

Answer on page 202

Question 146
Letter - Number Sequencing

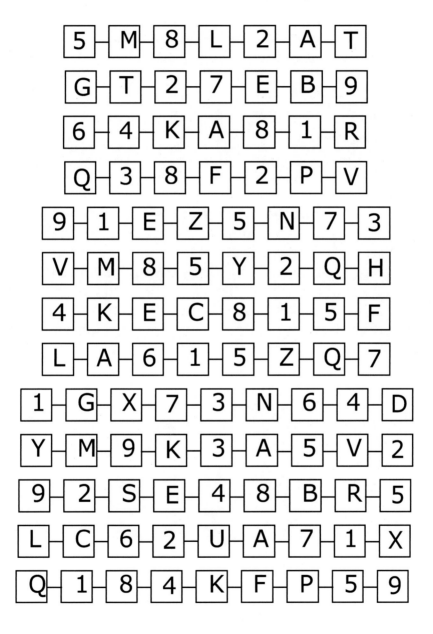

5 — M — 8 — L — 2 — A — T

G — T — 2 — 7 — E — B — 9

6 — 4 — K — A — 8 — 1 — R

Q — 3 — 8 — F — 2 — P — V

9 — 1 — E — Z — 5 — N — 7 — 3

V — M — 8 — 5 — Y — 2 — Q — H

4 — K — E — C — 8 — 1 — 5 — F

L — A — 6 — 1 — 5 — Z — Q — 7

1 — G — X — 7 — 3 — N — 6 — 4 — D

Y — M — 9 — K — 3 — A — 5 — V — 2

9 — 2 — S — E — 4 — 8 — B — R — 5

L — C — 6 — 2 — U — A — 7 — 1 — X

Q — 1 — 8 — 4 — K — F — P — 5 — 9

Picture Span Subtest
14 questions

Picture Span is a new subtest of Working Memory that assesses visual working memory. The child looks at a stimulus page with two or more pictures for a set amount of time before selecting the picture(s) (in sequential order) from options on a response page.

Instructions: Questions 147-160

1. For a few seconds, show the child a page with two or more pictures, and he/she must try to remember them in the same order.
2. The child should be shown the page of pictures on the following page and instructed to select the images he/she has seen and list them in the same order.
3. Do not show the child the previous page's pictures again.
4. Example: E, C

Answer on page 203

Question 147
Picture Span

1

2

A   B   C

D   E   F

1   2

Answer on page 203

Question 148
Picture Span

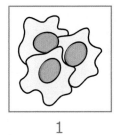

1   2

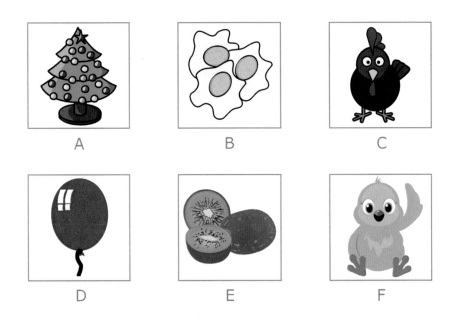

A   B   C

D   E   F

1   2

Answer on page 203

Question 149
Picture Span

1

2

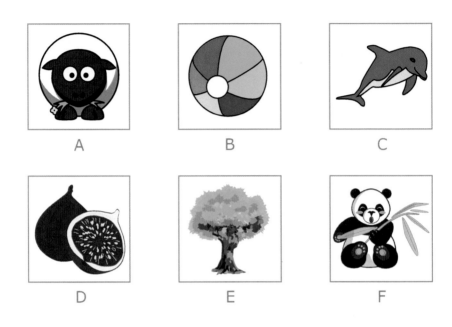

A B C

D E F

1 2

Answer on page 203

Question 150
Picture Span

1   2

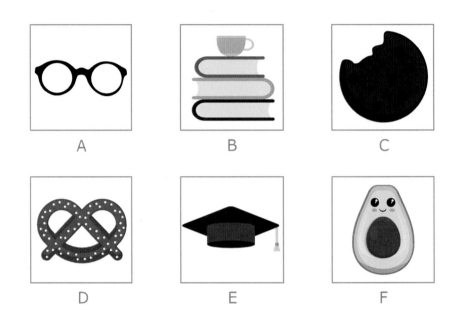

Answer on page 203

Question 151
Picture Span

1   2   3

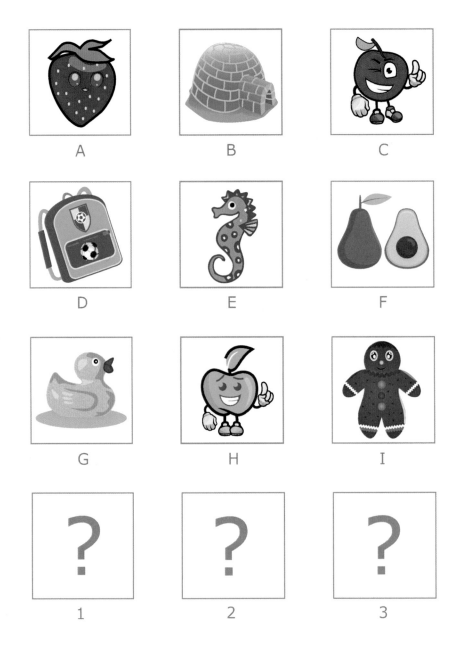

A

B

C

D

E

F

G

H

I

1

2

3

Answer on page 203

Question 152
Picture Span

1

2

3

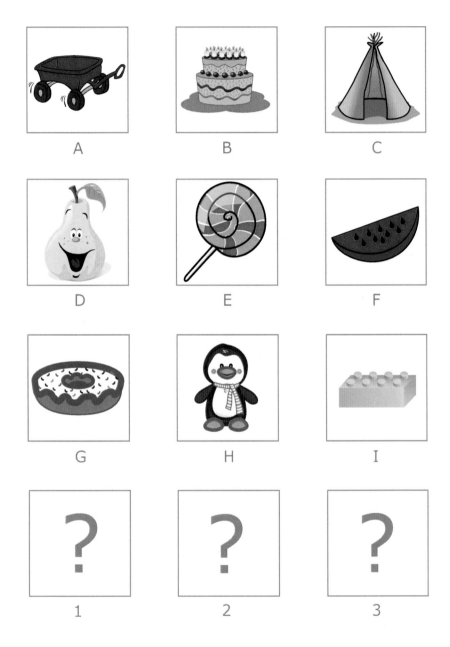

A

B

C

D

E

F

G

H

I

1

2

3

168

Answer on page 203

Question 153
Picture Span

1   2   3

A

B

C

D

E

F

G

H

I

1

2

3

Answer on page 203

Question 154
Picture Span

1   2   3

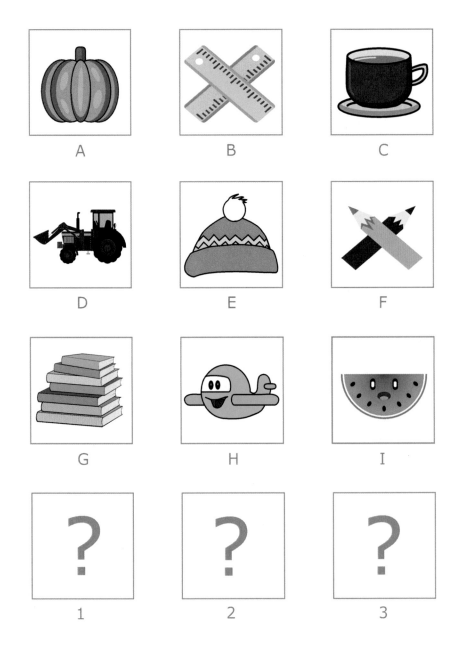

A

B

C

D

E

F

G

H

I

1

2

3

Answer on page 203

Question 155
Picture Span

1 2 3 4

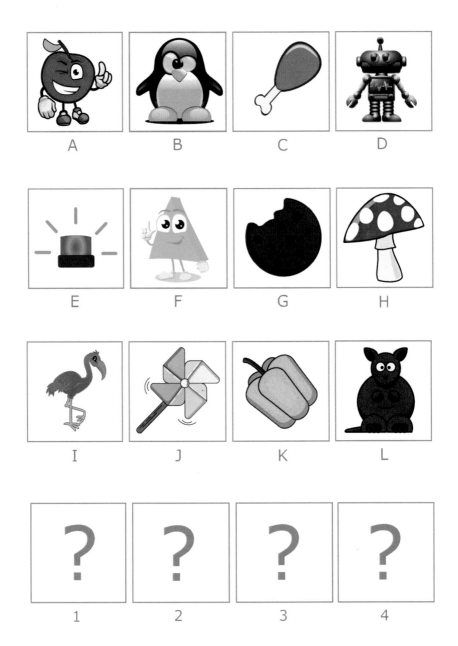

Answer on page 203

Question 156
Picture Span

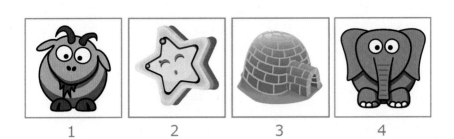

| 1 | 2 | 3 | 4 |

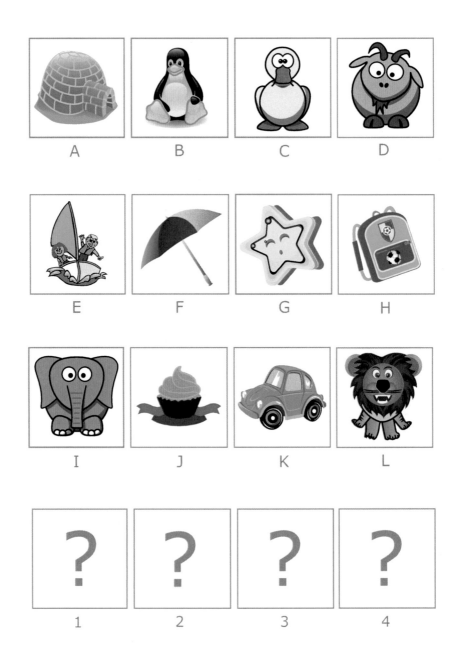

Answer on page 203

Question 157
Picture Span

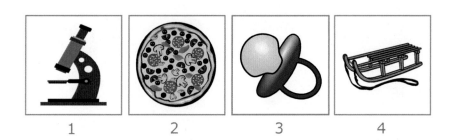

| 1 | 2 | 3 | 4 |

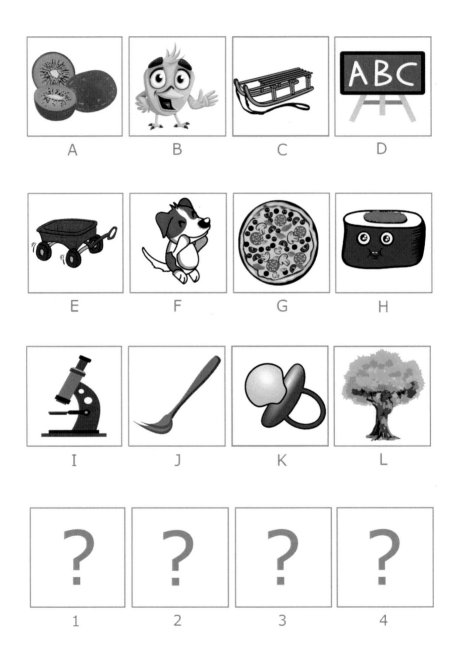

A

B

C

D

E

F

G

H

I

J

K

L

1

2

3

4

178

Answer on page 203

Question 158
Picture Span

1   2   3   4

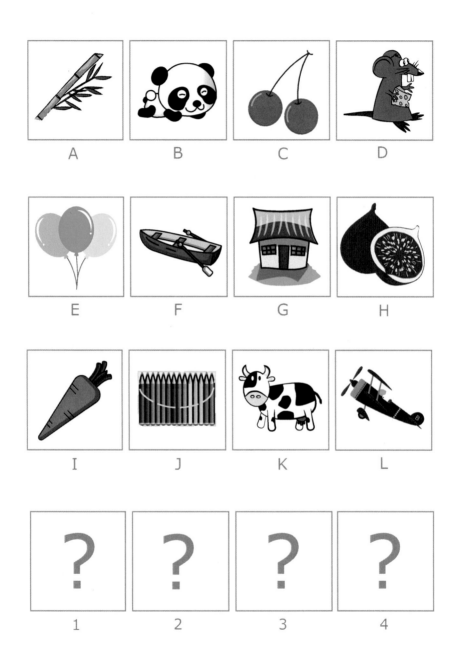

Answer on page 203

Question 159
Picture Span

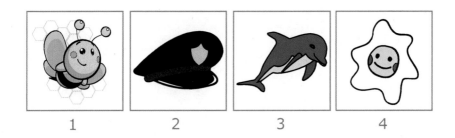

1   2   3   4

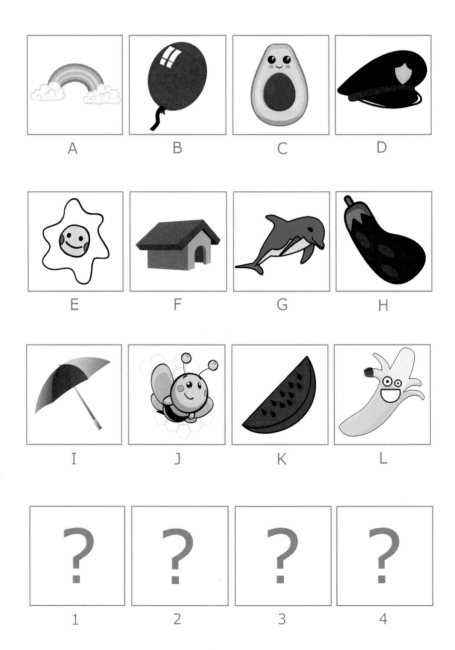

A   B   C   D

E   F   G   H

I   J   K   L

1   2   3   4

Answer on page 203

Question 160
Picture Span

Answers
Picture Concepts

1. Answer: A – Both are associated with babies.
2. Answer: B – Both are books.
3. Answer: D – Both are associated with eating.
4. Answer: C - A pacifier is used by the baby.
5. Answer: C – Both are furniture.
6. Answer: D - The book is kept in the library.
7. Answer: A - Both are concerned with art.
8. Answer: C – Both are public transport.
9. Answer: B - Both of them live on a farm.
10. Answer: B - Eskimos lives in igloos.
11. Answer: C - The dogs live in a kennel.
12. Answer: D - In the sandbox, you can use a shovel to play.
13. Answer: A - The egg is produced by the chicken.
14. Answer: A - Both are associated with Christmas.
15. Answer: D - Cheese is made from milk, which comes from cows.
16. Answer: B - Both are associated with a party.
17. Answer: D - Both are fast food.
18. Answer: A – Both are house.
19. Answer: C - Both are used in school.
20. Answer: A - Pandas eat bamboo.
21. Answer: C – All are used in school.
22. Answer: B - All of them are water sports.
23. Answer: D – All of them can fly.
24. Answer: A – They are all farm animals.
25. Answer: B - All have a round shape.
26. Answer: C - All are connected with the rain.
27. Answer: A – All are vegetables.
28. Answer: D - All of them are drinkable.
29. Answer: C – All of them are houses.
30. Answer: B - All of them have two wheels.

Answers
Picture Concepts

31. Answer: D - They all live in the forest.
32. Answer: A – They all live in the sea/ocean.
33. Answer: C - All associated with winter.
34. Answer: B - They are all related to a police officer.
35. Answer: D - All of them are eating utensils.
36. Answer: A – They are all plants.
37. Answer: A - They are all associated with the beach.
38. Answer: D - All of them produce milk.
39. Answer: B – They are all fast food.
40. Answer: C - All are associated with a doctor/ hospital.

Answers
Pattern Matrix Reasoning

41. Answer: D - The same figure appears in each row.

42. Answer: C - Each row has the same coloring.

43. Answer: A - Each row contains the same small and large figure. The colors of the two figures alternate.

44. Answer: C - The same figure appears in each row. The color of each column is the same.

45. Answer: D - The same figure and color appears in each row. In each box, the figures are rotated 180 degrees.

46. Answer: C - The color of each row is the same. The first figure is formed by combining the second and third figures.

47. Answer: D - Each row contains the same small and large figure.

48. Answer: A - The same figure appears in each row. Each row's figures rise by one in a clockwise direction.

49. Answer: C - Figures in each row increase by one, adding a smaller one. The first added figure is white, and the second is the same color as the other figures in the row.

50. Answer: B - The middle figure combines the left and right figures.

51. Answer: D - Each row's figure is rotated 90 degrees clockwise.

52. Answer: B - Each row and column in each figure has one horizontal, one vertical, and two cross lines.

53. Answer: A - Each row's figure is rotated 90 degrees clockwise. Each row contains one medium, one large, and one small figure.

54. Answer: D - The figures are moved counterclockwise in each row, reducing their number by one.

55. Answer: C - The figure's parts are increased by one in each row. The new parts have no color.

56. Answer: A - Each row contains the same small and large figures. The small figures in each row decrease by one clockwise.

57. Answer: D - The last figure from the top row disappears in the second box, and the first figure from the bottom row disappears in the third box.

58. Answer: C - The figures in each row decrease by one. The figures in the figure group's middle column disappear.

Answers
Pattern Matrix Reasoning

59. Answer: D - Each row has one large figure and two small figures. The large figure rotates 90 degrees clockwise, while the small figures move in the same direction.

60. Answer: A - The first and third columns contain the same large and small figures.

61. Answer: B - The figures in each row are moved down one position, with the bottom figure occupying the top position.

62. Answer: D - The figures in each row are increased by two. Vertically first, then horizontally. Figures with and without colors alternate.

63. Answer: C - In each row, the figures are alternately shaded and unshaded. The small colored figure moves diagonally while maintaining its color.

64. Answer: B - In each row, the figures are alternately shaded and unshaded. A triangle, square, and rhombus alternate in each row and column.

65. Answer: B - In each column, the three rectangles move clockwise. The long figure is shaded in the first column, the middle figure in the second, and the small figure in the third.

66. Answer: B - In each row, the arrow moves counterclockwise. Each time the triangle rotates 180 degrees.

67. Answer: C - Vertical, left-slanted, and right-slanted lines alternate in each row and column.

68. Answer: D - In each row, the figures are alternately shaded and unshaded. The small figure moves diagonally.

69. Answer: C - In each row, the small figures change their places counterclockwise. The triangle and square are always shaded, while the circle and square are never.

70. Answer: A - The third column is formed by combining the first two.

71. Answer: D - The third column is formed by combining the first two.

72. Answer: B - The small square moves one place counterclockwise in each row.

73. Answer: D - The large figure in the first column appears as small in subsequent columns, and the small figures appear as large. Color is the same way. The second and third columns have the same number of small figures as the first column.

Answers
Pattern Matrix Reasoning

74. Answer: D - Each row and column alternates between small, medium, and large figures. Each row has identical figures. The arrow rotates clockwise.

75. Answer: B - Each row has identical figures. The third column is formed by combining the first two.

76. Answer: C - Each row has identical big and small figures. The small figures (triangle, arrow and circle) move clockwise along the edges of the stars.

77. Answer: B - Each row has identical figures. One of the arrows in each row and column is rotated 180 degrees, and one of the rectangles is rotated 90 degrees.

78. Answer: B - Two opposing circles have been shaded. They proceed clockwise. Circles that were previously shaded become unshaded squares. This pattern continues on the next row.

79. Answer: A - Each row has identical small and big figures.

80. Answer: D - There is one vertical, one right-slanted, and one left-slanted line in each row and column. The circle moves counterclockwise through two of the star's edges. The pattern continues on the following row.

Answers
Naming Speed Literacy

81. Answer

Green frog	Blue bird	Red tomato	Blue car	Green watermelon	Yellow lemon	Red telephone
Green plane	Red apple	Green apple	Yellow banana	Red octopus	Green turtle	Red cherry
Yellow chicken	Yellow lemon	Green cucumber	Blue dinosaur	Red strawberry	Blue bird	Red fish
Green frog	Blue hippo	Red ladybug	Yellow sun	Green lemon	Red mushroom	Yellow duck
Blue star	Green mushroom	Yellow sun	Green pear	Blue fish	Blue robot	Red plane
Green snake	Red plane	Blue fish/ dolphin	Green tree	Red watermelon	Yellow pear	Blue fish/ whale
Red strawberry	Yellow pear	Red balloon	Blue robot	Green turtle	Red candy	Yellow lemon
Blue car	Yellow chicken	Blue bird	Red cherry	Green cucumber	Yellow banana	Red ladybug
Red octopus	Green turtle	Blue star	Green mushroom	Blue fish/ dolphin	Yellow duck	Red apple
Green watermelon	Red strawberry	Green plane	Yellow lemon	Red tomato	Blue fish	Blue dinosaur
Blue fish/ whale	Yellow lemon	Red candy	Blue hippo	Red plane	Green pear	Red plane

82. Answer

Red telephone	Yellow lemon	Green watermelon	Blue car	Red tomato	Blue bird	Green frog
Red cherry	Green turtle	Red octopus	Yellow banana	Green apple	Red apple	Green plane
Red fish	Blue bird	Red strawberry	Blue dinosaur	Green cucumber	Yellow lemon	Yellow chicken
Yellow duck	Red mushroom	Green lemon	Yellow pear	Red ladybug	Blue hippo	Green frog
Red plane	Blue robot	Blue fish	Green pear	Yellow sun	Green mushroom	Blue star
Blue fish/ whale	Yellow pear	Red watermelon	Green tree	Blue fish/ dolphin	Red plane	Green snake
Yellow lemon	Red candy	Green turtle	Blue robot	Red balloon	Green pear	Red strawberry
Red ladybug	Yellow banana	Green cucumber	Red cherry	Blue bird	Yellow chicken	Blue car
Red apple	Yellow duck	Blue fish/ dolphin	Green mushroom	Blue star	Green turtle	Red octopus
Blue dinosaur	Blue fish	Red tomato	Yellow lemon	Green plane	Red strawberry	Green watermelon
Red plane	Green pear	Red plane	Blue hippo	Red candy	Yellow lemon	Blue fish/ whale

Answers
Naming Speed Literacy

83. Answer

Green tree	Yellow lemon	Blue fish/whale	Blue dinosaur	Red cherry	Red plane	Blue star
Yellow chicken	Green turtle	Red octopus	Yellow lemon	Red fish	Yellow banana	Green snake
Green turtle	Blue bird	Green lemon	Red watermelon	Yellow duck	Blue dinosaur	Red strawberry
Red strawberry	Red tomato	Blue car	Red telephone	Red ladybug	Green snake	Blue car
Red candy	Green mushroom	Red strawberry	Blue fish	Green frog	Green pear	Red octopus
Yellow banana	Red plane	Blue dolphin	Green tree	Red plane	Yellow pear	Green watermelon
Yellow duck	Green apple	Red balloon	Blue robot	Green turtle	Blue bird	Blue fish/whale
Blue fish	Green cucumber	Blue bird	Red cherry	Green cucumber	Red apple	Green frog
Green pear	Red ladybug	Blue star	Green mushroom	Red mushroom	Yellow lemon	Green plane
Blue dolphin	Yellow sun	Green plane	Yellow lemon	Blue robot	Blue hippo	Yellow chicken
Red tomato	Yellow lemon	Red candy	Blue hippo	Red plane	Green watermelon	Red apple

84. Answer

Blue star	Red plane	Red cherry	Blue dinosaur	Blue fish/whale	Yellow lemon	Red mushroom
Green snake	Yellow banana	Red fish	Yellow lemon	Red octopus	Green turtle	Yellow chicken
Red strawberry	Blue dinosaur	Yellow duck	Red watermelon	Green lemon	Blue bird	Green turtle
Blue car	Blue star	Red ladybug	Red telephone	Blue car	Red tomato	Red strawberry
Red octopus	Green pear	Green frog	Blue fish	Red strawberry	Green mushroom	Red candy
Green watermelon	Yellow pear	Red plane	Green tree	Blue dolphin	Red plane	Yellow banana
Blue fish/whale	Blue bird	Green turtle	Blue robot	Red balloon	Green apple	Yellow duck
Green frog	Red apple	Green cucumber	Red cherry	Blue bird	Green cucumber	Blue fish
Green plane	Yellow lemon	Red mushroom	Green mushroom	Blue star	Red ladybug	Green pear
Yellow chicken	Blue hippo	Blue robot	Yellow lemon	Green plane	Yellow sun	Blue dolphin
Red apple	Green watermelon	Red plane	Blue hippo	Red candy	Yellow lemon	Red tomato

Answers
Naming Speed Literacy

85. Answer

Big yellow pear	Big red tomato	Small blue square	Big blue dinosaur	Big red cherry	Small red circle	Small blue circle
Big yellow chicken	Small green triangle	Big red octopus	Small yellow triangle	Small red square	Big yellow banana	Small green circle
Big green turtle	Small blue square	Small green triangle	Big red watermelon	Small yellow circle	Small blue triangle	Big red strawberry
Small red circle	Big red tomato	Small blue circle	Big red telephone	Small red triangle	Big yellow pear	Big blue car
Big red candy	Small green square	Small red circle	Small blue triangle	Big green frog	Small green circle	Big red octopus
Small yellow square	Big red plane	Small blue square	Small green square	Small red circle	Big yellow pear	Small green triangle
Big yellow duck	Small green square	Big red balloon	Big blue robot	Small green circle	Small yellow triangle	Big blue fish/whale
Big blue fish	Small green triangle	Big blue bird	Small red square	Green cucumber	Small red circle	Small green square
Small green circle	Big red ladybug	Small blue circle	Big green mushroom	Small red square	Small yellow triangle	Big green plane
Big blue dolphin	Small yellow square	Big green plane	Big yellow lemon	Small blue circle	Small blue square	Big yellow chicken
Small red square	Small yellow triangle	Big red candy	Big blue hippo	Small red triangle	Big green watermelon	Small red circle

Answers
Naming Speed Literacy

86. Answer

Small blue triangle	Small red square	Big red cherry	Big blue dinosaur	Small blue circle	Big blue fish/whale	Big yellow pear
Small green circle	Big yellow banana	Small red triangle	Small yellow circle	Big red octopus	Small green triangle	Big yellow chicken
Big red strawberry	Small blue square	Small yellow triangle	Big red watermelon	Small green circle	Small blue triangle	Big green turtle
Big blue car	Big yellow pear	Small red square	Big red telephone	Small blue square	Big red tomato	Small red circle
Big red octopus	Small green circle	Big green frog	Small blue circle	Small red triangle	Small green triangle	Big red candy
Small green square	Big yellow pear	Small red circle	Small green triangle	Small blue triangle	Big red plane	Small yellow circle
Big blue fish/whale	Small blue triangle	Small green square	Big blue robot	Big red balloon	Small green circle	Big yellow duck
Small green triangle	Small red square	Big green cucumber	Small red circle	Big blue bird	Small green triangle	Big blue fish
Big green plane	Small yellow circle	Small red triangle	Big green mushroom	Small blue square	Big red ladybug	Small green triangle
Big yellow chicken	Small blue square	Small blue circle	Big yellow lemon	Big green plane	Small yellow square	Big blue dolphin
Small red square	Big green watermelon	Small red triangle	Big blue hippo	Big red candy	Small yellow circle	Small red circle

Answers
Naming Speed Literacy

87. Answer

```
5 P W 8 1 N S 9 6 4
E A 2 L F 3 7 X C K
6 8 Y D 1 Z 5 U 6 G
J T 4 C O R 7 1 I A
H 2 N M 9 S T 6 P 7
K L 5 1 4 K Q R P 3
F X N 6 M 3 9 K B U
L 6 4 2 W 1 C A 8 4
Q 7 Y 3 P V X 1 6 3
Y C 2 Z I T 3 2 E R
J L F 5 3 7 1 G D S
```

88. Answer

```
R S 2 P 5 9 L H G Z
4 6 J T 1 M D 6 C 2
1 Q V 5 N 9 V B 5 9
X 4 E 7 J L W U 6 4
2 9 3 G S 4 Q K 5 U
Z 5 8 T X 6 B 8 N E
K Y P 4 9 1 C S 6 3
J P G I 5 7 D 8 H 1
8 O T P S V 4 2 9 4
K B 9 V 2 Z 7 E M S
6 Q K F 6 8 C Y 1 7
```

89. Answer

```
6 P w 5 1 7 S 9 6 4
E A 2 L F 3 7 x C K
6 8 Y d 1 Z 2 U 6 G
j T 3 C o R 7 1 i a
h 2 n M 9 S T 6 p 7
k L 5 1 4 K Q r P 2
f X N 6 M 3 8 K b U
l 6 3 2 W 1 C a 8 4
q 7 y 3 P v X 1 6 3
Y C 2 z I T 8 2 e R
J L f 9 3 7 1 g D S
```

90. Answer

```
r S 8 P 5 3 L h g Z
2 6 J T 1 m D 6 C 2
7 q V 5 N 9 V b 6 1
X 4 E 7 J L w U 6 3
5 9 3 g S 7 q K 5 U
Z 5 8 T X 6 B 8 N E
K y P 4 9 1 c S 6 8
J P g I 5 7 d 8 h 1
2 O t P S v 1 2 9 7
K b 9 V 2 z 7 e m S
4 q k f 6 5 C Y 1 9
```

Answers
Naming Speed Quantity

91. Answer

4	2	1	2	2	1	2
3	4	1	1	2	2	3
2	2	1	2	1	5	2
4	1	3	3	1	2	3
2	4	2	2	3	2	2
1	3	2	3	2	2	3
1	2	4	2	1	3	4
3	2	1	1	3	2	4
2	2	3	2	2	3	2
4	2	1	2	4	2	1
1	2	2	2	1	2	4

92. Answer

2	3	2	2	3	2	2
1	2	4	2	1	2	4
4	2	1	2	2	2	1
4	3	1	2	4	2	1
4	2	3	1	1	2	3
2	5	1	2	1	2	2
3	2	1	3	3	1	4
2	2	3	2	2	4	2
3	2	2	3	2	3	1
2	1	2	2	1	2	4
3	2	2	1	1	4	3

93. Answer

2	4	2	1	2	1	2
4	3	1	1	3	2	2
2	2	2	1	2	5	1
1	4	3	3	3	2	1
4	2	2	2	2	2	3
3	1	3	2	3	2	2
2	1	2	4	4	3	1
2	3	1	1	4	2	3
2	2	2	3	2	3	2
2	4	2	1	1	2	4
2	1	2	2	4	2	1

94. Answer

2	5	1	2	1	2	2
3	2	1	3	3	1	4
2	1	2	2	1	2	4
3	2	2	1	1	4	3
4	3	1	2	4	2	1
4	2	3	1	1	2	3
2	2	3	2	2	4	2
3	2	2	3	2	3	1
1	2	4	2	1	2	4
4	2	1	2	2	2	1
2	3	2	2	3	2	2

Answers
Naming Speed Quantity

95. Answer

1	3	4	1	2	4	2
3	2	4	3	2	1	1
2	3	2	2	2	3	2
4	2	1	4	2	1	2
1	2	4	1	2	2	2
2	2	1	2	4	2	1
1	2	3	3	3	4	1
2	1	5	2	2	2	1
3	1	2	3	4	1	3
2	3	2	2	2	4	2
3	2	2	3	1	3	2

96. Answer

4	4	3	5	3	4	4
3	1	2	3	4	3	1
3	2	4	2	3	4	3
5	2	5	4	1	3	5
2	3	3	3	5	2	5
5	5	4	3	2	4	2
4	4	1	3	2	1	3
2	4	3	2	5	4	1
4	3	2	3	5	3	4
2	5	1	3	4	3	2
4	2	4	3	1	3	5

97. Answer

4	4	3	5	3	4	4
1	3	4	3	2	1	3
3	4	3	2	4	2	3
5	3	1	4	5	2	5
5	2	5	3	3	3	2
2	4	2	3	4	5	5
3	1	2	3	1	4	4
1	4	5	2	3	4	2
4	3	5	3	2	3	4
2	3	4	3	1	5	2
5	3	1	3	4	2	4

98. Answer

5	5	4	3	2	4	2
4	4	1	3	2	1	3
2	4	3	2	5	4	1
4	3	2	3	5	3	4
2	5	1	3	4	3	2
4	2	4	3	1	3	5
4	4	3	5	3	4	4
3	1	2	3	4	3	1
3	2	4	2	3	4	3
5	2	5	4	1	3	5
2	3	3	3	5	2	5

Answers
Naming Speed Quantity

99. Answer

5	3	1	4	5	2	5
5	2	5	3	3	3	2
2	4	2	3	4	5	5
2	1	3	4	4	1	3
5	4	1	2	4	3	2
5	3	4	4	3	2	3
2	3	4	3	1	5	2
5	3	1	3	4	2	4
3	5	3	4	4	4	4
2	3	4	3	1	3	1
4	2	3	4	3	3	2

100. Answer

4	4	3	4	4	3	5
3	1	4	3	1	2	3
4	3	3	3	2	4	2
3	4	1	5	2	5	4
2	5	5	2	3	3	3
4	2	2	5	5	4	3
1	3	2	4	4	1	3
4	1	5	2	4	3	2
3	4	5	4	3	2	3
3	2	4	2	5	1	3
3	5	1	4	2	4	3

Answers
Immediate Symbol Translation

101. Answer: You love to play golf
102. Answer: You like to come here
103. Answer: I love the smell of cake
104. Answer: I like to cook with you
105. Answer: I like to drink cold water
106. Answer: It is very cold outside today
107. Answer: You are going to school today
108. Answer: That is a very small school
109. Answer: I like to play that game
110. Answer: That is a very small ball

Answers
Delayed Symbol Translation

111. Answer: play, love
112. Answer: to, golf
113. Answer: like, cake
114. Answer: I, of, cook
115. Answer: smell, you, the
116. Answer: cold, drink, with
117. Answer: water, small, it
118. Answer: is, today, outside
119. Answer: very, are, going

Answers
Delayed Recognition

120. B
121. D
122. A
123. A
124. D
125. C
126. B
127. C
128. A
129. D
130. B
131. A
132. C
133. D
134. A
135. B
136. A
137. D
138. C
139. C
140. B

Answers
Digit Span

141. Answer:

1,4
6,2
5,3,7
8,0,9
4,3,7,5
2,6,1,9,4
0,8,3,7,6
1,7,5,0,9,2
8,3,1,0,5,9,4
6,2,4,7,0,3,5
9,1,8,2,7,6,3,0
2,5,7,4,8,0,9,1,3
1,8,6,2,9,5,3,0,4

Answers
Digit Span Backwards

142. Answer:

7,5
1,3
4,0,9
8,2,6
6,7,5,1
4,8,3,0,9
9,6,1,5,2
1,9,7,2,6,4
9,6,4,8,5,3,0
0,5,2,3,7,8,1
2,8,4,1,9,0,5,6
3,6,7,0,8,1,4,2,9
2,7,4,9,3,8,6,1,5

Answers
Digit Span Sequencing

143. Answer:

1,4
2,6
4,5,8
0,7,9
1,2,4,6
0,3,5,8,9
2,4,5,6,7
0,1,4,5,8,9
2,3,4,5,7,8,9
0,1,3,4,6,7,8
0,2,4,5,6,7,8,9
0,1,3,4,5,6,7,8,9
0,2,3,4,5,6,7,8,9

Answers
Letter - Number Sequencing

144. Answer:

2,D
5,A
6,B
8,H
1,M
7,K
3,P
4,5,F
2,9,S
3,7,L
9,N,V
4,6,U
2,E,R

Answers
Letter - Number Sequencing

145. Answer:

3,8,K,P
1,4,T,Q
5,7,W,X
2,9,B,J
2,4,8,N,S
3,5,6,D,H
5,8,K,R,V
1,2,A,Q,T
3,5,7,B,S,U
4,6,7,C,G,I
2,3,9,A,E,J
1,6,8,F,V,Z
3,4,8,M,P,R

146. Answer:

2,5,8,A,M,L,T
2,7,9,B,E,G,T
1,4,6,8,A,K,R
2,3,8,F,P,Q,V
1,3,5,7,9,E,N,Z
2,5,8,H,M,Q,V,Y
1,4,5,8,C,E,F,K
1,5,6,7,A,L,Q,Z
1,3,4,6,7,D,G,N,X
2,3,5,9,A,K,M,V,Y
2,4,5,8,9,B,E,R,S
1,2,6,7,A,C,L,U,X
1,4,5,8,9,F,K,P,Q

Answers
Picture Span

147. E,C
148. B,D
149. F,E
150. D,A
151. I,E,C
152. C,B,D
153. F,E,B
154. H,I,G
155. J,I,G,B
156. D,G,A,I
157. I,G,K,C
158. H,K,C,F
159. J,D,G,E
160. L,G,J,E

**Thank you for your purchase!
I hope you enjoyed this book!**

Please consider leaving a review!
https://prfc.nl/go/abreview

*Please don't hesitate to contact us
if you have any questions!*

e-mail: info@prfc.nl